D1085925

Contents

PROLOGUE

I'd sit on the street curb where Eggleston St. tees into 104th St., right in front of my best friend's house, Paulie Hernandez; 104 streets south of the center of downtown Chicago and 3 ½ blocks east of Halsted St. in the community of Roseland. I spent the first 8 years of my life there and it was about as far as you could go on the south side of Chicago.

I was just a tyke, but I could spot a 1963 Chevrolet Impala from 300 yards away and it didn't matter if it was day or night. The headlights gave it away every time. And there was only one 1963 Chevy Impala that headed north on Eggleston where it tees into 104th St., my Dad's.

It was the first car I can remember my dad owning. He'd be up, showered, dressed, out the door, and working for hours before I, my sister, and two brothers even got out of bed. So, at the end of many summer days, I'd sit on the curb in front of Paulie's house waiting to see the headlights of my Dad's car. Those headlights heading home always made me happy as a little kid. Maybe not so much when I got older and my mom would warn, "Wait till your dad gets home!", after one of us screwed up.

I just loved hanging out with my Dad. He was the strongest, wisest, hardest working, most athletic man this little guy ever saw.

He was also the Store Manager of High Low Foods on 111th and Halsted. By the time I was 9 or 10, I was the Shopping Cart Manager of High Low Foods on 111th and Halsted. My responsibilities included helping people with their groceries, shagging shopping carts, and returning them to their rightful spot back in the store. For my hard labor on hot summer days, I was paid $10.00 for 9 to 10 hours of work, which I promptly spent on record albums by the checkout counter. My Dad would also give me a few bucks to grab two Quarter Pounders with cheese for us from the McDonald's down the street. I was living large, let me tell ya.

I didn't do it for the money, I did it to hang with my Dad. The side benefit to that was that it sure got me off to a good start in terms of my vinyl collection. I still have those first records from High Low Foods.

Besides the grocery store industry, my Dad and I shared the love of Chicago sports teams. I can remember with uncanny detail watching hockey games on our 19" black and white TV with my Pops. Whoever were my Dad's favorite players, were also my favorite players because my Dad knew best. Bobby Hull, Stan Mikita, Tony Esposito, Pit Martin, Dennis Hull, Whitey Stapleton, and Jimmy Pappin made up some of the best hockey teams that never won a Stanley Cup. But we lived in Chicago and in Chicago at that time, championships by any of our teams were few and far between.

We never made it to a Blackhawk game back in the 60's or 70's, but we sure did go to our fair share of Cub's games. I couldn't believe my eyes when I saw Wrigley Field, in person, for the first time. I fully expected to walk into that old ballpark and see black and white uniforms and playing turf because that's what I always saw on our TV. It was truly a technicolor explosion when I first saw the green grass, the beautiful Ivy on the outfield walls, Cubbie blue and red, and the hated Cardinals red uniforms. I was like a kid on a Tilt-A-Whirl, head spinning with excitement. Better yet, I was in Wrigley Field with my Dad seeing the backs of Lou Brock's and Curt Flood's jerseys while Williams, Santo, and Banks smacked baseballs all over the Friendly Confines. Unless, of course, Bob Gibson was pitching because we rarely beat Gibson. It was always the Cardinals and we always sat in the Bleachers. It's how we did it. We weren't Bums though. My Dad and I were baseball purists.

I was always a better fan than I was a player. I tried my best, but my exceptionally poor vision made it next to impossible to hit a round baseball with a cylindrical bat or judge the path of a flyball. It wasn't until I ditched the Coke bottle glasses, at age 17, for contact lenses that sports got easier for me. That's ok. We all have our strengths and weaknesses, but that never stopped my Dad from playing catch with me, or my two brothers. It didn't matter if he just worked a 65-hour week or more, by the second or third pleading he would have that right-handed glove on and teaching us the finer points of America's pastime.

This is a perfect example of my Dad's unselfishness besides giving up his R&R time to have a catch with us. He's left-handed. He was born a southpaw and he still is to this day. But he never had a left-handed mitt. He played in the street, and on the field, with a right-handed glove and somehow made the transition from catching the ball in his left hand, removing the glove, tucking it under his arm, and throwing the ball with that same left hand as smoothly as Cubs' shortstop Don Kessinger would turn, jump, and throw a perfect strike to Banks from deep in the hole between short and 3rd.

Why did he do this? Because all we had in the house were right-handed gloves and he made do with what we had. He had larger fiscal responsibilities than buying a glove for himself. He's as old school as there is. He had kids to feed, with one trying to eat him out of house and home, as I was often told. School supplies, food in the fridge, kid's shoes, broken glasses every 6 months, a mortgage, kid's tonsil removal and eye operations are where his focus steadfastly remained.

Later in my teens, I worked with my Dad again. I wanted to go to college because that's what my friends were doing. My Dad gave me a golden opportunity to earn money to pay for this school of higher learning. So, I became a cook on Amtrak in the summer of '78. I made a ton of money and saved most of it for Northern Illinois University. I had three main routes – New York City, Los Angeles, and Seattle. It was one hell of an experience for an 18-year old kid. We'd get a day layover in each city with Amtrak picking up the tab, while putting us up in nice hotels. There's a lot a teenager could do on his own, in the late 70's, in Los Angeles and New York City. And I did.

My Dad jumped through a lot of hoops to get me this job and after two years, I thanked him by unceremoniously quitting without notice. I was sitting in Chicago's Union Station on what we called "Station Protect". Your job is to go there and sit and wait to see if someone doesn't make it in for their scheduled trip. If that happens, you take their place.

You don't know if you're going or when you're going and at the time, I was really struggling with the job. I was, for all intents and purposes, handed the job because of my Dad's influence. The old railroad guys that worked on the train their entire lives weren't crazy about this arrangement and some of them did all they could to make my trips difficult. And I was the kind of kid that never backed down. Never. There was more than one occasion where fights were broken up between me and some older guy because I refused to take what they were giving.

So, I quit. Right then and there in Union Station without bothering to let Amtrak know, not a good idea.

I wasn't sure how this would play out with my Dad, but I was certain I handled the situation as wrong as I possibly could. I was 18 and clearly not mature enough to handle this like an adult. I screwed up because of fear mostly. I was afraid I was going to give someone a severe beating or some old cook was going to stab me in the chest with a butcher knife.

When I saw my Dad that evening, he was shocked and disappointed. How could he not be? He had people he had to answer to for my actions and for that, I felt terrible. But it never became an ongoing problem for us. He never held it against me, and it was in our rearview in no time. That's how my Dad is. He'll get mad and he will just as fast, move on from it with those he loves. You see, he loves all of us unconditionally and my guess is that he didn't let anyone at Amtrak talk bad of me, although they had a right to. He didn't come right out and say this to me, but he knew I was an immature kid with a bad temper. It took a while for me to get a handle on that, but it never stopped my Dad from being in my corner and for that, I'm eternally grateful.

I've tried to instill that same work ethic in my daughters that my dad instilled in me. I'm certain I had little to do with it but all three of them are in much better place personally and professionally than I was at their age. They crushed it in high school and college compared to me crushing beer cans on my forehead in high school and college. It was different time.

Today, my dad isn't doing well. His body is almost 88 years old and it's suffering the consequences of a difficult childhood on the southside of Chicago, enlistment in the Korean War at the age of 17 in which he earned a Bronze Star and Purple Heart, followed by a career in which he worked long, hard hours to provide for my mom, my brothers, my sister, and myself.

When I think of my dad, I think of a guy that was always there for me, always had my back, and always doing all he could to help me and that was no easy trick sometimes. I think we'd all agree that I've been the most difficult for my parents. I've always been a challenge compared to Joe, Kathy, and Bill in that regard. I'm wired differently than they are, and my Father walked side by side with me as I untangled that mess.

This is for you, Dad. I am eternally grateful for your kindness, wisdom, direction, and love. I miss you.

One more thing – I haven't been working in boiler rooms or on hydronic systems my entire career, just the best part. Like most people of this trade, I've serviced or installed standard air conditioning systems, high velocity air conditioning systems, ductless mini-splits, belt-driven Low Boy furnaces, to high end 95% AFUE condensing furnaces, humidification and dehumidification systems, exhaust fans, and make-up air units. I've fabricated and installed hundreds and hundreds of custom-made sheet metal fittings and have the scars to prove it.

I taught a couple of HVAC classes at the local community college, worked HVAC technical support, and when I first started out, I'd do anything they told me to do. I swept floors, cleaned the shop, helped guys clean their trucks, run for parts, deliver parts, and my boss even had me cut his grass a few times. I didn't care. $4.50 an hour is $4.50 an hour no matter how you slice it.

But nothing blew my hair back like boilers, near boiler piping, and radiant panel heating systems did. I dabbled with it in my early career, until I went all in some time in the early to mid 90's. Much of that I owe to Dan Holohan and the books he wrote. He sparked an interest in me that still shines bright today. Stories of Levittown, the Great Pickle Puzzle, and Steam Heating systems pulled me in hook, line, and sinker. I couldn't get enough of it.

Thank you, Dan. I may have been knocking tin together my whole life without you.

CHAPTER 1 – I'll Take the Blame

Or, at least, my fair share of it.

The guy who trained and managed me in my early days was 10 years my senior. His name was Larry and he stood 6'4", weighed 240 pounds give or take a bacon double cheeseburger, and was about as charming as a starving grizzly bear. His name has been changed to protect the innocent; me.

He drank his weight in Old Style by early afternoon, but it made him less homicidal, so I really didn't mind.

Every now and then I would make a wildly unpopular suggestion that I shouldn't have to buy his beer because I'm only getting paid $4.50/hour. His typical response was that at $4.50/hour, the bosses were grossly overpaying me. This was usually followed by a reminder that my job was to make his job easier.

The thing that was always hardest for me was that he could never wrap his giant-sized head around the fact that I couldn't do things as well, or as fast, as he could. He, despite his elevated blood alcohol level, was oddly, very good at what he did. Or so it seemed to a 20-year old kid with 3 1/2 weeks of experience. Yes, weeks.

I was already a tough kid, but he tested my resolve and made me tougher. If I couldn't slip a drive cleat on two lengths of rectangular duct in five seconds or less, he was right in my face saying, "What in the $&@! is so hard about that!?" Then he would knock me out of the way and slip on the cleat faster than I could pick myself up off the floor.

My singular goal in life was to shut him up. Because if I did, it would mean I'm getting better. After a couple of years of unrelenting torture and abuse, we were producing at the same pace with similar results. He still drank on the job. I saved mine for after work doing my best to blot out his disdain for my day's efforts.

The thing is, I liked the guy. He was charming in his own monstrous way. He made me a better technician and taught me so many things; the tricks of the trade if you will. Not long after we worked together, I was a union tin knocker for Local 73 in Chicago. That was kind of a proud moment for me and I owe much of my eye for detail, and the need for productivity, to him. I also owe some of my over-the-top, micromanagement skills to him. Not all, but some.

Being a nostalgic type guy, I smile when I think back to all the jobs we worked together in my early days. He taught me well. Too well, perhaps.

His management skills were sorely lacking and mostly nonexistent.

Ten years later, mine were no better.

Larry was born in 1951 and I was born in 1960. I guess that makes us Baby Boomers and not once have I ever heard us described as the greatest generation ever, so cut us some slack. We did the best we could on what we were taught and how we were managed. That was never a problem until I became a manager of people.

At some misguided moment in 1987, I decided I was just about the most gifted serviceman/installer this industry had ever seen. And when you're blessed that kind of talent, the next obvious step is to quit your well-paying, benefits ridden job, hang up a neon sign, and open my own shop. Right?

Wrong.

But I did anyway.

Let me run through all the good stuff first. I may have exaggerated my other-worldly technical skills, but I was relatively good at what I did and always had the grey matter entrenched in a technical manual or textbook. I loved to learn, still do.

I developed a strong, loyal customer base that included light commercial work and residential. I never considered myself a salesman, but I sold more than enough work by sharing references and previous job before and after pictures; a portfolio, if you will. Integrity and honesty were on my side too.

We lived in a nice house and our young daughters could pick out as many books from Barnes & Noble as their little, but curious, brains desired. There was never a cap on the books they wanted so long as they read them. Three kids, a golden retriever named Mikey, a minivan that I loathed, a tricked-out work van and a brand, spanking new three car garage. We even went on vacation every year.

Life was good.

And then, I hired my very first employee. It started out as an exciting new part of my business. The business was growing, and I needed help. I recruited him from a local supply house. He had just about everything you could ask for in a young kid; intelligent, reliable, conscientious, and teachable. He showed up for work every day and his effort should have never been in question, but it was. Enough was never enough for me.

I'm sharing this because maybe it will help steer a young buck or two in the right direction. It might even change an old tradesman/entrepreneur like I was. I came to terms with this a few months ago when it finally, after 3 decades or so, became as obvious as a broken coupler and sagging motor mounts on a three-piece Bell & Gossett circulator. This epiphany was so dramatic that it even made the same sound as that coupler banging against the housing at 1725 revolutions per minute.

There was a problem and that problem was me. It mostly revolved around my inexplicable inability to manage people with any modicum of sustained sanity. This mad method of management cost me dearly in terms of employee turnover. Here's a short list of people who worked for me starting from the beginning.

Bill, Pete, Ray, Mark, Dan, Jim, Brian, Scott, Mike, Eric, Michael, Evgeni, Alex, Ralph, Tom, Sammy, Johnny the Bull, Danny, Steve, and Tim. That's like Matt Damon reciting the names of his 13 imaginary brothers in Good Will Hunting. Jeez!

20 guys, and I'm sure there's more than a few that I forgot. Among these hostages were my younger brother, my neighbor's 18-year old kid, one of my best friends, and my son-in-law.

The longest tenured technician lasted 2.5 years. TWO POINT FIVE YEARS over the course of 30 years. Ouch. That stings a little bit, but I've heard that admitting you have a problem is the first step. I considered that Step 1. The turnstile under my neon sign was busier than the local Walmart on Black Friday.

Don't get me wrong, there were some good times. Good conversations, hearty laughs, and light moments. They were often abbreviated good times, but you got to take what you can get. I paid them well and on time, kept them busy, taught them to be better technicians and installers, gave them a truck to use, and provided benefits. But if you think that's all it takes to retain good employees, and most of them were good, we need to have a conversation. Let my experience save you from the eventual chest grabber that you're bound to have should you follow my path.

The biggest problem I had was expectations. I expected everyone to have the same drive, the same attention to detail, the same yearning for more and more knowledge, and the same immaculately organized and maintained truck. The same, same, same. You'd think I was running a cloning business instead of a heating business. Expectations, they say, are inversely proportional to happiness. I wasn't happy much of the time and an unhappy boss can only lead to one thing, unhappy employees.

I'm not suggesting you throw out the company handbook and let havoc reign supreme. I am suggesting you not be the strictly black and white guy that I was, allow for some grey in the picture. Everyone's brain and way of thinking and seeing things is uniquely different. Hire the right people, continue training them, trust them, allow them to make mistakes, and then provide a learning opportunity for them.

Show respect. Always. Even if you must terminate them, do it respectfully. And if they terminate you, respect their choice.

Be empathetic. Everyone has a life outside of work and employers barely have a glimpse of what that is.

Listen. Their body language often speaks louder than words. If their actions or words tells you there's a problem. Intervene. Don't ignore them or you'll lose them. Talk it through and work it out.

Apologize. If you screw up, man up.

Be patient. I can't stress this enough.

Give praise every time its due.

When you must criticize, do it constructively and in private. Being calm probably isn't going to kill you either, although I wouldn't know because that was a tactic I rarely tried.

Granted, there must be some strict, unbreakable rules like not being under the influence of Old Style beer at 1:25 pm on a Tuesday afternoon while driving your truck.

If you have a guy like the Larry mentioned above, lose him. Or get him in a substance abuse program as a condition of employment. If you don't, you could end up in a world of hurt and a living nightmare of litigation.

Stealing is another one that no company should abide. The Dude does not abide. I'd explain the reference but that would make me as lame than the reference itself.

Unexcused absences, being excessively late every single day, using the truck without permission are some other behaviors that can't be tolerated.

But if you have a guy with great enthusiasm, suits up and shows up every day, gives his best effort, is great with customers, and does a good job; back off. Now. Right now. Cut him as much slack as you possibly can with things that at the end of the day, simply do not matter.

Forget about choosing your battles wisely. What matters are your choice of words and actions. That's where the wisdom comes into play and those are the things that will define you as a leader and manager.

Don't manage people like Larry and I did, because if you do it will end badly. Nobody wants to work for that guy.

The job is tough but, as managers, we must be the most professional ones in the room.

The concept is simple.

The execution is difficult.

CHAPTER 2 – It'll Never Work

That's what they told me. They warned me and they told me not to do it. They said I'm wasting my time and my customer's money and that they'll never realize any energy savings. They said the radiators are going to leak because you'll be operating at system pressures infinitely higher than the old system. They also said the new system will never provide enough heat because the heat output of the radiators will be so low that Mr. and Mrs. Jones will be calling you in the dead of winter, at 1 am, because your fancy new system with all the bells and whistles, just isn't able to heat their home like the old boiler did. Mrs. Jones won't be happy and when she's not happy, nobody's happy. Mr. Jones will suggest you get in your truck right now, hightail it over there, and make this thing right before she gives him the boot.

The "they" that I speak of are the most passionate hydronic installers and technicians in the country. They have arms like Goliath from swinging 3' and 4' steel pipe wrenches all day and from hauling cast iron boilers in and out of trucks and up and down stairs. They understand their systems better than anyone. They abide by The Lost Art of Steam Heating, Dan Holohan's masterpiece, as if it were etched on stone tablets by a power greater than themselves. They have nicknames like Steamhead, Steamwright, and Ezzy T. They are the Steam Boiler Experts. They know the potential pitfalls better than anyone. So, I heeded their warnings. I listened to them and even took notes. Then I went to work, keeping what they taught me in mind.

The job that I was asked to provide a bid for was at an old church, built in 1895, in historic Lemont, Illinois. Their steam boiler had failed, leaking from the sections like a sieve. They had more pipe repair clamps throughout the building than I've ever seen. On average, I'd estimate 1 clamp for every foot of pipe. If the steam system were to remain, all the piping throughout the church would have to be replaced. It was obvious that it had never been properly maintained or cared for and that's a shame because a properly set up steam system is a beautiful thing.

Bethany Lutheran Church

I based my design/bid on the fact that I wanted to install a very efficient system that will keep the pastor and her congregants toasty all winter long without issue, and without disrupting the building's unparalleled integrity. My plan was to remove the steam boiler and all of it's piping except the radiators that can be converted to hot water, install 2 modulating condensing boilers, and run two 1/2" Pex-Al-Pex pipes to each radiator and connect them to manifolds in the boiler room. For a radiator to be converted from steam to hot water, it must be connected across the top and the bottom and 4 of them in this church were not. I was sure to make note of that and include new radiators in my proposal. Every steam guy out there probably wants to stop reading this right about now. I challenge you not to.

At this point I'm not certain my solution is viable. I must do the math and trust the math to make sure my design will perform up to, and beyond, expectations. The first step is always a Manual J Heat Loss Calculation to determine just how much heat the building is losing, and then compare it to the Equivalent Direct Radiation (EDR) of the heat emitters throughout the church. The latter calculation will tell me how much heat each heat emitter can deliver with both steam and hot water. This is critical because steam is capable of 240 BTU/h per square foot of radiation whereas hot water tops out at about 170 BTU/h per square foot of radiation based on 180 degrees water. When added all up, that 70 BTU/h difference per square foot between steam and hot water is the key that makes or breaks the deal; keeps them warm or lets them freeze.

The hardest part of doing a heat loss calculation is making sure you gather accurate information from the building. Inaccurate information being fed to load calculation software is going to spit out inaccurate numbers, resulting in improperly sized equipment. Garbage in, garbage out as the saying goes. Compounding errors is another way to look at it. So, I spent the better part of the day measuring outside walls, windows, doors, insulation, building material, floor square footage, ceiling square footage, and making some educated guesses based on what the church told me and what I know about construction after 38 years in the field. The envelope of this church would be considered loose at best. Old windows, very little insulation, doors with air gaps, etc. The easiest part is the work back at the office where all I must do is plug in the information and let the software do the heavy lifting.

The EDR calculation is something I still do by hand but is just as effective. It starts with your list of radiators, their height and width, number of columns or tubes, and the total number of sections for the radiator. The illustration below shows the chart and the steps to calculate EDR.

I'm encouraged by the results I'm getting. The total heat loss for the sanctuary and the meeting room below it came to 253,086 BTU/h. My connected load, or EDR, of all heat emitters came in 333,560 BTU/h based on the 180 degrees water temperature. I have significantly more radiation than needed to meet the heat loss. This means my hottest supply water temperature ever needed will be below 180 degrees. In any hot water heating system, the lower the return water temperature, the more efficient it is. With modulating condensing boilers there is no limit to how low we go. The lower, the better. For this system, we use a 20 degrees design difference between the supply water and the return water temperature. It's not an exact science but it gives us a target. Therefore, if we're delivering 180 degrees water to the radiators, we can expect 160 degrees return water temperatures under steady, stable conditions.

Just how efficient are we going to be? From Step 3 in the chart above, you'll see that we get 170 BTU/H/SF at 180 degrees water temperature. Again, we have 333,560 BTU/h which is equivalent to 1962 EDR. The math is so straightforward even I can get it. 333,560/170 = 1962. Taking it one step further, look at the chart below. This gives us the BTU/H/SF and their corresponding supply water temperatures.

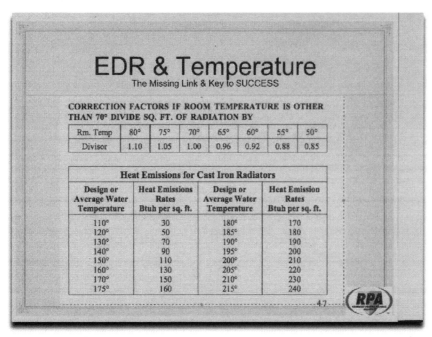

Courtesy of the RPA

Here's how it breaks down for the church:

SWT	EDR x BTU/H/SF = Total BTU/H
160 degrees	1962 x 130 = 255,060 BTU/h
150 degrees	1962 x 110 = 215,820 BTU/h
140 degrees	1962 x 90 = 176,580 BTU/h
130 degrees	1962 x 70 = 137,340 BTU/h
120 degrees	1962 x 50 = 98,100 BTU/h
110 degrees	1962 x 30 = 58,860 BTU/h
100 degrees	1962 x 10 = 19,620 BTU/h

As you see, we will be able to heat the church with 160 degree supply water temperature on the coldest day of the year because the heat loss is only 253,000 BTU/h and change. That will give us 140 degrees return water temperature which gets us close to the flue gas condensing mode of 135 degrees. This is playing out about as well as I could have hoped for. It's only the coldest day of the year for one day so these boilers, properly sized, are going to be in condensing mode much of the season. That's exactly what you want from a mod con boiler. If we weren't going to be in condensing mode most of the time, I would have suggested sticking with steam. But now I know with absolute certainty that the operating efficiency of the boilers will be significantly higher than a steam boiler. It gets even better. The equipment I proposed was two floor standing boilers with 10:1 modulation turndown ratio. Paired and cascaded, that means the turndown could be as high as 20:1. Steam boilers can't do that.

Based on my design, the detailed presentation I gave the church council, and the fact that we just hit it off I was awarded the job. That was 2 years ago. Everything has gone well the first two winters. There were some adjustments needed for the outdoor reset control until we hit the sweet spot for their comfort level but that is to be expected on most jobs. I also had to twist their arms a little along the way to remove the radiator covers which cut down on the heat output significantly. I pressure tested each radiator at 25 PSI prior to connecting them to the new homerun manifold distribution system. We had 2 leakers right off the bat and none since then. I consider that a win. I forewarned them that we may have a few that need to be replaced. While we pressure tested them, we also flushed each one removing all the rust and debris from what was left of the steam system. Drilling and tapping each radiator for the manual coin vent went as smooth as silk. We had a drop ceiling on the lower level where my guys were able to, neatly and quickly, run the new PAP supply and returns to each radiator. The manifolds in the boiler room had flow meters and valves for adjusting so we were able to dial in the flow to each radiator based on its size.

It's rare that these conversions make sense, but I had a feeling the first day I looked at the system that this might be one of them. I did the math and trusted the math. The steam guys taught me everything I needed to know to avoid the mistakes that can and do happen if you're not diligent. The icing on the cake was that our company won the Lochinvar VIP Installation Showcase for this job. That always brings a smile to my face.

Lochinvar Fire-Tube Boilers

CHAPTER 3 - Hockey, Writing, and Wiring

All I wanted to be when I was a kid was a writer, a sportswriter. But not just a sportswriter, I wanted to be a beat writer for the Chicago Blackhawks hockey team. I imagined myself in a smoke-filled newsroom, chomping on a cigar, my fedora tipped back, crumpled up pieces of paper strewn across the floor after being ripped from my old Corona typewriter, and finger punching letter keys that would soon become a story. Back in the day, then owner Dollar Bill Wirtz would not televise any home games because he was certain it would hurt ticket sales at the gate. To make things even worse for us stay-at-home fans, he wouldn't even allow radio coverage of the 1st period for the same reason. Nobody loved the Blackhawks more than I did and I listened to every minute available; every Lloyd Pettit call went straight from his mouth to my ears and my job would be simple. I would tell the tale of every Bobby Hull slapshot, Stan Mikita maneuver, Keith Magnuson fight, and every great save by Glenn Hall or Tony Esposito to everyone who wasn't fortunate enough to visit the venerable building at 1800 W. Madison Street, Chicago Stadium. I was just a little kid, but my mind was made up. I was going to be a writer.

How I pictured myself as a kid.

The best laid plans of mice and men often go astray, or so I'm told. Grade school, high school, and a relatively brief stint in college got me no closer to my goal. Next up was HVAC trade school at Coyne

American Institute; an old, brick building on Fullerton Avenue on the north side of Chicago. It was there that my career path was no longer in doubt. My future as a pipe fitter, tin knocker, and service technician was secured. I picked up the tools, went to work, and liked it so much that I stuck with it for the next 38 years. I've been an installer, serviceman, adjunct faculty at a community college, HVAC technical support specialist, and a mechanical contractor. Eventually, it got to the point where my body could not take a single more beating. Wrenching 3" pipe, hauling boiler blocks or sections up and down stairs, loading and unloading, and crawling around in places where old guys aren't meant to go takes its toll after a few decades or more. I stayed in the trenches longer than most and for that I'm grateful.

I then went to work for a nonprofit organization in Chicago called Elevate Energy. Our goal was simple and basic, smarter energy use for all. We implemented programs, provide direction, support, and oversight of energy upgrades for income eligible nonprofit organizations, multifamily buildings, and single-family homes across all communities of Chicago. This gig got me inside boiler rooms without having to lift anything heavier than a combustion analyzer. I didn't think I could be happier or more fortunate. And then PHC News called. They asked if I'd be interested writing a column for them. What? Me? A writer? My knee jerk reaction was two-fold…yes! And, are you sure you want me? PHC News was already my favorite trade magazine. Harvey Ramer is hands down, my favorite new writer. Hot Rod and I go way back to the early days of heatinghelp.com and has always been somebody I've looked up to and respected as one of the pillars in the hydronic industry. His imagination and ability to think outside the box is second to none. Just like that, I became a writer. It feels good and my hope is that a young technician or two will learn something from what I share.

The one topic that comes to mind right away is the electrical and control work on residential and light commercial applications. In my experience, this seems to be an afterthought to some and just a nuisance to others. On larger commercial work, it's not unusual for the installing company to have its own electrical crew(s) or to just subcontract the work to an electrical contractor. I think this is an area where we could do better.

We've all seen our fair share of botched jobs. They usually start with cutthroat pricing, a lack of knowledge, an unwillingness to learn, no design, and a Three Stooges "A Plumbing We Will Go" plan of attack. There's no good way this ends. The completed job is painful to look at, the system doesn't perform as promised, and the customer ends up overpaying for lowball number. That being said, from what I've seen through the years most jobs are acceptable, but nothing that will make the building owner invite friends over, prop chairs in front of the boiler, pop a beer, and stare in awe at the beautiful sight before their eyes. It's a boiler and it heats the place.

The next type of installation that I commonly see is the one where the company does **almost** everything right. The proposed cost of the job is fair and profitable. If you want to stay in business, you must make a profit. Profit is not a bad word. It's part and parcel to keeping your doors open and your company thriving. The design started with a Manual J based, heat loss load calculation so that the boiler is sized to match the heat loss of the building; followed by equipment selection, piping strategy and schematic, control strategy and schematic, pump sizing, and a clear plan of attack on how the job will executed. 3/4 of the way through the job everything is looking picture perfect. Boiler is hung level on the wall or set on the floor on a housekeeping pad. The piping is plumb, level, properly supported, with professional looking soldered joints or clean pipe dope joints. The venting uses the proper pipe with the correct pitch and is terminated per manufacturer's recommendations and local code. The boiler's condensate line is piped with PVC and includes a condensate neutralizer kit. Gas pipe is sized correctly, plumb, level, and secure. It has a gas shutoff, union, and a drip leg. The relief valve is piped vertically with a discharge pipe within inches of the floor. If they could stop right now the job would be considered grade A, top shelf, and maybe one that John Seigenthaler would include in the next edition of Modern Hydronic Heating.

Unfortunately, it's not finished yet. There's one, seemingly simple task that still needs to be completed. It's the one that comes near the end of the job, near the end of the day, when everyone's tired, and the one where the ball gets dropped more times than not. THE ELECTRIC. Line voltage to the boiler(s), pumps, and relays. Low voltage control wiring to or from the thermostats, sensors, relays, and safety related devices. It's here where we see extraordinary lengths of BX and greenfield and other various forms of flexible cable weaving in a dizzying, crisscross, over under sort of way. There's usually no rhyme or reason as to why it was done that way. It just was. And there's seldom a piece of 1/2" EMT, electrical metallic tubing, in sight. Black Sharpie lettering is the preferred method of labeling and if a mistake is made, no worries, scribble it out and start again. All the line voltage wires are black and white; as if blue, yellow, orange, and red wires didn't exist. The low voltage control wiring is a rat's nest of unlabeled, 18-gauge wire, redefining the Temptation's Ball of Confusion. When you remove the boiler's cover and see this, all you can offer at first is a thousand-yard stare of sadness knowing what you're up against.

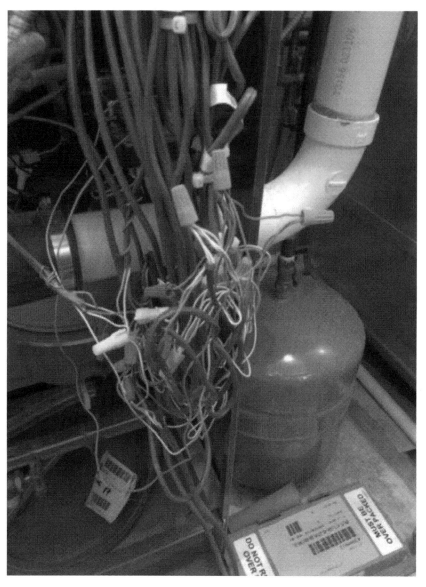

What a mess!

It doesn't have to be like that. There are much better, cleaner methods of wiring that can make installations and future troubleshooting easier. Proper wire management, the ability to make a few simple bends with 1/2" conduit, following the National Electrical Code, professional looking labels, using zone valve controls and pump controls, a few tips and tricks here and there, and your electrical work will be on par with your incredible boiler design and piping skills. It's also a great way to differentiate yourself or your company from others who are comfortable with the bar not being held so high. We're all wired differently but our boiler rooms don't have to be. Most of my jobs have look identical to one another. Once I find a way that works, I tend to stick with it until I find a way to improve on it.

The professional look.

This picture is from an apartment building job we did a few years ago. It's about 95% complete at this point. I opted for a wire trough, the long horizontal box beneath the circulators, on this one because of the number of pumps. I knew it wouldn't look good without it and for the little bit of extra cost, it was an easy choice for me. There's also a second pump relay, not pictured, to the upper left of the hydraulic separator. It was much easier to do this than to have longs lengths of greenfield and ½" conduit. I loved the way it looked too.

CHAPTER 4 – Wiring for Success

Let's take a look at the iniquities of poor control wiring and what to do about it.

Ten years ago, I walked into this mechanical room in the Beverly neighborhood of Chicago. It wasn't just any mechanical room though. It was the mechanical room in the home of a City of Chicago Police Department Captain. You don't get to be a police captain by accepting mediocrity or, in this case, epic failure. And I'm not sure I've seen anything worse than what you see here. It's unsafe, sloppy, unprofessional, and in terms of effort and execution, about as bad as it gets. It ought to be illegal.

Just brutal.

This was not a work in progress. This was a job that some installer deemed complete. It had been this way for about 8 years when I laid eyes on it. The piping may be even worse than the wiring, but that's another story, for another day. We're focusing on the wiring for now.

I have no issue with the multiple pump relays that were used or the disconnect switches for each pump. The use of independent switches was a good idea. The things that make me cover my eyes in horror are the duct tape labeling, dangling switches, the spaghetti mess of low voltage wiring, lack of tie straps, no plan, little skill, and minimal effort.

It does not have to be like this. Ever. The picture below is one that I did, in the same era, using similar components. For me, it's easier to do it the right way. The 1900 boxes are level and on the same plane, the pump relays are level and on the same plane, there are 6 identical EMT (electric metallic tubing) offsets going from the switches to the pump relays. Once you make one, the other five are a breeze. The spacing between the boxes are all the same. The knockouts that are used are kept consistent to make it look like you planned it that way because you did. A plan is where every successful job begins. The low voltage wire is either hidden or "telephone corded" to add another professional touch to it. "Telephone-cording" is easy. Just wrap your 18-2 or 18-4 low voltage wire, tight and condensed, around the shaft of a long, Phillips screwdriver. Once you've got enough wrapped to cover your run from Point A to Point B, just slide it off the screwdriver. A flat blade screwdriver won't let you do that.

My work from the mid-90's.

The reason I used older controls for this example is to show you that even with multiple controls and boxes, you can make it look clean with a bit of forethought and some practice.

Proper wire management, the use of stake-on connectors, raceways, EMT, a torpedo level, working from a wiring schematic, professional labeling, conduit box offsets, anti-short bushings, 6' maximum lengths of greenfield, using wire strippers to strip wires so you don't nick them, twisting the wires with linesman pliers before spinning on a wire nut, "telephone cording", tie straps, and the right clamps will improve the wiring on any boiler, furnace, or air conditioner job put before you.

The electric is typically one of the last things you do on an installation, but you can't treat it like a political conversation over Thanksgiving Dinner. The wiring can't be avoided. It must be done, and if you're going to do it, you may as well do it right. Right? Makes sense to me. My dad used to say to me, "If you don't have time to do it right the first time, when are you going to find the time to do it a second time? Because that's exactly what you're going to do now." Ouch.

I spent many decades in the trenches, so I get it. You're on your third, sweat soaked T-shirt and that same sweat is burning your eyes, and the air you're breathing is like inhaling dried oatmeal. Your boss is pushing you to finish the boiler install because he wants you to do a service call on your way home. We've all been there. It's as familiar as your favorite pipe wrench.

This is the point where we need to ignore the noise and do our job. **Ignore the noise. Do your job.** I borrowed that little saying from one, very successful NFL coach. I liked it so much that there's a Post-It Note of it stuck to my computer.

We live and work in the age of social media where Walls of Shame are appearing everywhere. You don't want to be part of that motley crew and there's no reason you ever should. I'm going to do my best to help you avoid that.

First things first, get organized. If you're not running back and forth to the truck every 10 minutes, you're going to make things much easier on yourself. You'll be more productive and you'll feel confident you have everything you need to get the job done in a timely manner. The boxes below are just a glimpse into how organized I like things. I don't even start the electric until all the gas piping is done, leak checked, and all its gear back on the truck. In addition to the Milwaukee boxes, I'll bring down my electrical tools, wire, conduit, and greenfield. It's like starting a new job.

Secondly, use the right tools for the task at hand. I like to use a portable bandsaw to cut both the conduit and the greenfield (armored flexible conduit). It's lightening quick, easy, and makes square cuts. My arms are big enough. I have no desire to use a hacksaw anymore.

If you're using linesman pliers or needle nose pliers to strip wires, stop. You may be stripping more than the wire insulation. Gauged wire strippers are easier to use, and you'll only cut what you want to cut. There should always be a marker, pencil, tape measure, and torpedo level on your belt. A pocket flashlight and a non-contact voltage detector are staples for me as well. Before commissioning the equipment, you'll need to break out the multi-meter to confirm voltages beyond what the non-contact detector is capable of.

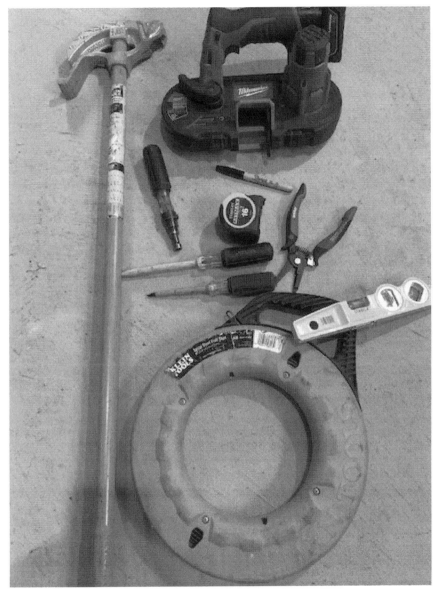

Tools of the trade.

Next, learn how to bend conduit. If you can pipe-fit a boiler, chances are you can bend conduit with the best of them. I can usually get in and out of most boiler rooms by knowing how to execute just a couple of bends. The most common bends are the box offset, and the 90 Degree Stub. And everything I refer to will be using 1/2" EMT, as it's the pipe and size most often used in boiler room applications.

Let's start with the box offset. This is the pipe that's going in to, or out of, an electrical box. The box knockout for the pipe is raised 3/8" above the mounting surface so we need to bend the pipe to accommodate this offset. For the longest time, I just eyeballed these bends and it looked ok. Then I learned how simple it was to do it by the book, and I never looked back. Exactness is not a bad thing.

The most common electrical box I've used is referred to as a 1900 box, 4" wide x 4" high x 1.5" deep. 1900 Box, strange name isn't it? I looked it up once and found that the original electrical box this size was a Model 1900, so the name just stuck. Go figure.

There are only a few things you need to remember when bending a box offset. 3", 2 1/8", and 10 degrees. That's it. If you remember those three things, you're golden. On a straight piece of 1/2" conduit, mark a point 3" from the end of the pipe with a marker. This will be the spot for your first bend and gives us just enough meat to get our bender on it. Wrap the mark all the way around the pipe because you'll need to see if from different angles.

From that mark, measure and mark a second spot 2 1/8" down from the 3" mark and wrap it all the way around the pipe just like the first one. This point represents our offset. When you're done, the pipe will look like this.

Box offset markings.

This is easier than you thought it would be, isn't it? I thought the same thing. We only have a couple steps left and then we're done. This is where the 10 degrees comes into play. There are three specific symbols on your conduit bender. A Teardrop (or Notch), a Star, and an Arrow. In the picture below, the Arrow is on the far left, the Teardrop (or Notch) is in the middle and the Star on the far right. For the box offset, we're only going to use the Arrow. With the handle end of your bender resting on the floor, place the pipe into the bender hook with the first mark at 3" lined up with the Arrow. It's just a coincidence that the second mark lines up with the Star. Don't let that confuse you. I'm right-handed, so I have my right hand on the pipe. My left hand is on the bender and my left foot is holding the handle of the bender in place at the floor level. Like so:

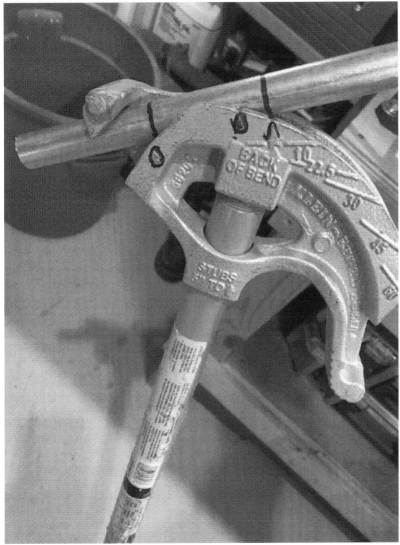

First bend of a box offset.

At the right of the Star, you'll see designated degrees of bends. 10, 22.5, 30, 45, and 90 degrees. You're going to push down with your right hand until the pipe is parallel with the 10 degrees line. The first bend is now complete. Now flip the pipe over and line the second mark up with the Arrow. Make certain that your pipe is straight in the bender otherwise your two bends will be on different planes. Push down again until you're, once again, parallel with the 10 degrees mark. Your offset is now complete.

2 marks, one at 3" and the other 2 1/8" from that. To keep it simple, I mark at 3" and 5 1/8" every time. Line up first mark at Arrow, bend to 10 degrees. Flip the pipe over and repeat, making sure bends are at the same plane. Sweet, right? Note: I only used a marker for this demonstration. Using a pencil I a much better option.

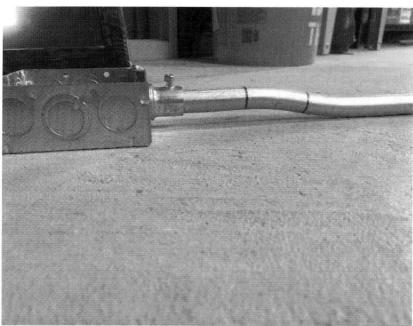

Less than 15 seconds to the correct offset.

Next up is the 90 Degree Stub. This smooth move will get you from a horizontal or vertical run of pipe, 90 degrees into a box or fitting without even the thought of guessing. Some simple math and execution and it will look like you sub-contracted Sparky's Inc. to do it for you.

Let's say you have the top of a box mounted 48" above the finished floor. You want to come out the top of that box with 1/2" conduit and bend it 90 degrees, so it's running horizontal 64" A.F.F. Some things you need to know:

- The Arrow symbol is also used for 90 degrees stubs.

- 1/2" EMT has a "take-up" of 5" when bending the pipe to 90 degrees.

- The difference between the top of our 1900 box and our horizontal run of pipe is 64" – 48" = 18".

- You'll be working with your pipe and bender at the floor, using your foot to execute the bend rather your hand.

- Keeping the 5" take-up in mind we must mark our pipe, from its end, at 13" to get the required 18" bend.

- Simply insert the pipe into the hook of the bender on the floor, align the 13" mark with the arrow, and exert pressure on the heal of the bender with your foot until the pipe is bent to 90 degrees.

- That's it!

The internet is full of information and videos of how to bend conduit. Many of us are visual learners so don't discount visiting YouTube for instructional videos. There are also free calculator apps available for bending pipe that will provide you with the take-ups, deductions, and suggested angles for different bends. At times, you may see some numbers that are slightly different than mine like a 1/16" of an inch or so. Don't sweat that too much. In fact, don't sweat it at all.

Rules that I follow for Flexible Metallic Conduit (Greenfield):

- I prefer to keep my whips to 4' or less, but most jurisdictions will allow up to 6'.

- I cut it with a portable bandsaw. Again – lightning fast, clean, and square.

- Always use the red anti-short bushings. I like to use the ones with the tails, they make it easier for the inspector to find them.

- Don't skimp on the one-hole straps keeping the uniform, secure, and professional looking.

- From your pump relays to your pumps, don't be afraid to use most of the run with 1/2" EMT and then a 3/8" whip using the appropriate adapter fitting.

- Please note the difference between Greenfield and BX. Greenfield does not come with wire in it and on very short lengths, you can pull additional wire through it. BX comes with wire in it, you can't pull through it, and most places where I've worked, it's against code. I never use BX.

- Use a ground wire on loads that require one. Always.

- When it makes sense, consider a wire trough like I mentioned earlier.

Rules that I follow for Low Voltage Wiring:

- Whenever you can, hide it. Tie strap on the back side of conduit or gas pipe. The less you see, the better.

- Consider the use of low voltage terminal strips within equipment panels, near the controls, instead of wire nuts. This method makes troubleshooting easier and comes with a professional look.

- I "telephone-cord" just about every length that is not tie-strapped to a pipe unless that length is 4" or less.

- Before you disconnect any low voltage wiring on equipment, label it so it's easily identified when it needs to be reconnected. Don't rely on color codes alone.

- If you're going through a knockout with it, make sure you use a grommet to avoid shorts.

Labeling

As mentioned earlier, I'm not a fan of using a marker for labeling. I use a Brother P-Touch Labeler. I'm sure it's outdated already but my point is that you've really got to use one if you want to make a favorable impression with your customers. It also helps everyone involved to connect the dots in terms of what's going on.

I label the boilers Boiler 1, Boiler 2, and so on.

I label pump relays, zone valve relays, pumps, zone valves, transformers, low water cut-offs, acid neutralizer kits, flow switches, mixing valves, exhaust pipe (if it's Class IV), intake pipe, Snowmelt controls, etc.

Once you start labeling, you can't stop. It becomes a sickness that may, at some point, require intervention.

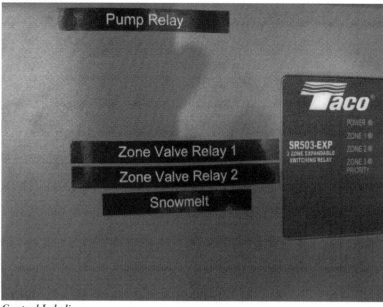

Control Labeling.

If you have any control wiring outside the boiler cabinet that does not come as part of the boiler itself, please leave behind a Wiring Schematic along with a Sequence of Operation. This an absolute necessity so the next poor soul who comes along isn't required to do any hydronic calculus to understand what your intent was.

I didn't always do things the right way or the best way. I had to be taught just like all of us do. Together, let's keep raising the bar.

C H A P T E R 5 – Servicing Modulating Condensing Boilers

When you're in the mod con boiler business, you need to take your technical acumen to the next level, or you won't be in the mod con business for long.

I can't tell you how many times someone has told me that they've had their boiler serviced every year since it was installed 5 years ago but, as of late, they've starting to have problems with it. Invariably, as soon as I pop the panels and access the heat exchanger, it becomes clear as a brand new sight glass that it's never been serviced properly. Don't be a ripping and running service tech like those guys. They're a dime a dozen. Differentiate yourself. Do it like you want to be considered among the best. Go big or go home.

Be Ready.
Before I begin working on these boilers, there are few things I like to have in order first. Being prepared is a great way to start anything.

I like to have a copy of the installation manual and service manual with me for that specific boiler. It can be a hard copy or a document you've saved on your phone or iPad. A Weil McLain Ultra Series 3 isn't the same as a Lochinvar KHN and that's completely different from a Triangle Tube. You may not need it but if you do, you'll be glad you followed this suggestion.

Make sure you have the right tools and test instruments with you. Here are some of the things I make sure are represented in my bad a$$ Veto Pro Pac tool bag: a can of compressed air, clean cloths, grit cloth, a N95 mask, OEM replacement burner gaskets, Ph test strips, metric and standard ball end Allen wrenches, metric and standard nut drivers, metric and standard gear wrenches, magnetic tray, TDS strips, pH strips, multi-meter, soft brush, flashlight, and inspection mirror. I like to wear a headlamp as well. Having the light follow your head movement makes too much sense not to.

The other obvious tools that aren't going to fit in your tool bag are a small shop vac, and a properly calibrated combustion analyzer with printer.

Ready to dig in?

Check the fault history.
The reason for this is simple. If there's something amiss with this piece of equipment, you're going to want to know about it before you pick up a tool. The manufacturer's give us this tool to be used to our advantage. Use it. Taking a snapshot of the screen with your phone isn't a bad idea either. The more you document, the better.

Access and clean the heat exchanger.
It's only six words but don't let that fool you. There's some work involved here and the first time on any specific boiler is going to be a lesson that can't be learned any other way but getting your hands dirty. Don't let that stop you. Once you do it, nobody can take that knowledge away from you and the second time will be infinitely easier. You're likely going to be removing the combustion blower, gas valve, cover plates, sight glasses, igniter, and sensor with each of them having a gasket that's going to want to rip to shreds the second you touch it. Go slow and easy removing them.

During this process, that magnetic tray will be your best friend. Most of those screws you'll be removing won't be something you're going to have on your truck. Lose one and your day just went from promising to anxiety ridden search for a 1 in 1000 screw.

For the actual cleaning part, I'm going to refer you directly to the manufacturer's instructions. They tend to be specific on how to attack it and we don't want heat exchanger warranties being voided because we did this when they asked for that. Follow the manual. That's why we have it with us.

That said, I've used CLR, a green Scotch-Brite pad, and a damp cloth with good results. Then I flush it with water until the water coming out of the drain is clear.

Dirty heat exchanger.

Clean heat exchanger.

Clean burner if applicable.

Be careful here. You don't want to damage it and you don't want it damaging you. This is where your mask becomes your MVP of tools. Wear it and maybe some nitrile gloves. Some of the ceramic fibers may be carcinogenic when overheated. Don't take the chance, and again, follow manufacturer's recommendations.

Gently pull the burner.

Clean flame sensor.

It needs to be clean and it won't be when you get there, I guarantee it. I typically use light steel wool to shine it up. I also inspect the ceramic part of it to make sure there aren't any hairline cracks in it. If there is, do your customer and yourself a favor by replacing it. It's part of why we're there, to prevent future problems.

Clean electrodes and check gap.

Use the same procedure here as the flame sensor for cleaning; and check manufacturer's suggested gap, usually 1/8".

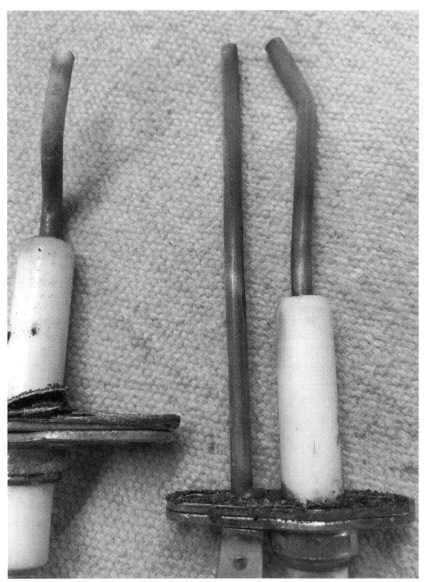

Ignitor and sensor in need of service.

Inspect HX gaskets.

The gaskets need to be intact. It's that simple. If they aren't, the combustion process will not perform as intended. That's why I always try to keep a bunch on hand. They're inexpensive but become very expensive if you have to make a run to your supply house in rush hour traffic, snow on the road, and technicians are backed up four deep at the counter and it just happens to be the same day where everyone's order is a minimum of 25 line items. We've all got decent size work trucks. Let's make sure were stocking them with the little things that don't take up much space and usually aren't readily available. I'd bet I replaced a gasket on every third mod con, at minimum.

Perform combustion analysis and adjust gas valve, if necessary, to meet manufacturer's specifications. This is where things get real. It starts with a quality, properly calibrated combustion analyzer. I use a Testo 320 because I did my homework before buying one and this is one of a few that got consistently solid reviews. The graphics are appealing, and it comes with a printer. You'll want to leave documented results of your analysis, so the next technician has a historic record of the burner's performance. It's also reassurance for your customer that you've done your due diligence.

The burner should be checked at both low fire and high fire after running for at least 15 minutes; a steady state is what the engineers like to call it.

Most boiler manufacturers provide a test port for your analyzer probe but if there isn't one, you'll have to provide one. I drill a 1/4" hole, run a pipe tap through it, and use a stainless steel plug when I'm done. Using a piece of tape is unprofessional in my opinion and potentially unsafe. Erring on the side of caution is the best option in this case.

Now anyone can turn on an analyzer, insert a probe into the flue pipe, and press print after a few minutes. It's what you see in those results that can separate you from the pack. Is it burning lean? Burning rich? Can you tell, either way, by looking at the CO_2 or the O_2? How does the excess air look? Is the amount of CO being produced within an acceptable limit? Flue gas temperature where it should be?

Here's what I know, and I'd like to share it with you.

Chemistry students and chemical engineers like to throw around the term stoichiometry when talking about combustion. **Stoichiometric combustion**, they say, is a theoretical position in which the optimal amount of oxygen and fuel mix generates the most heat possible and maximum combustion efficiency is achieved. The key word there is "theoretical". Theoretical as in it's not going to happen; not in my boiler, your boiler, or any of your customer's boilers. It can't because it would require using 100% oxygen. We don't use 100% oxygen and we never have. We use 100% air and air is made up of only 20.9% oxygen and 78% nitrogen with the balance made up of a variety of gasses. Stoichiometry isn't really my thing but, of this, I'm certain.

Back to the actual analysis, I want to see the results fall within the range set forth by the manufacturer. I wouldn't know those unless I opened and read the manuals. I even use a highlighter. I am a heating geek to the nth degree. I love digging in and reading the stuff that most techs don't think they need to, or don't think they have the time for. They're wrong on both accounts. Of this, I'm also sure.

I also know that O_2 and CO_2 are inversely proportional to one another. What the heck does that mean?

That's what I said the first time I heard it to. Once I wrapped my head around it, I knew that it meant that If the O2 is high, the CO2 is going to be low. And if the O2 is low, the CO2 is going to high. If O2 is somewhere in the middle, CO2 will be lurking in the same neighborhood.

If O2 is high, you're burning lean. You have too little gas (underfired) or too much air.

If O2 is low, you're burning rich. You have too much gas (overfired) or too little air.

If your excess air is too high, your efficiency is going to suffer.

If your CO is high, a lot more than efficiency is going to suffer.

I know that it's essential to do a combustion analysis on every start up and on every annual maintenance call.

Don't underestimate the number of resources available to you for further combustion analysis knowledge. I encourage you to engage in them. Try YouTube first. Tru-Tech Tools has several great videos using Bacharach, Testo, and other analyzers. Step by step stuff that won't leave any questions unanswered.

Ray Wohlfarth has spent much of his life in boiler rooms and his books won't let you down. Much of the content deals with CO, CO2, O2, excess air, combustion efficiency, CO free air, and flue gas temperatures. My favorite is <u>Lessons Learned Servicing Boilers</u>.

Heatinghelp.com's "The Wall" will have all kinds of information on combustion analysis shared by some of the brightest people in our industry. Just type what you need in the search box and wait for the fields to populate. Jim Davis may be the foremost authority on the subject, and he hangs out there regularly.

And don't overlook the obvious; analyzer manufacturer's websites have excellent videos and PDFs that can be downloaded for future reference.

Adjust control parameters to better fit the type of system if necessary.
When setting up the control parameters you must have, at least, a basic understanding of the system the boiler is serving, its occupants, and your local weather.

Is it a high temperature system? Cast iron radiators, cast iron baseboard, fin-tube baseboard, fan coils, and the like would fit this category.

Is it a low temperature system? Radiant floors, walls, or ceilings are the culprits here. High mass or low mass? Can it recover from setback temperatures?

Setting the Outside Reset numbers is, for the most part, simple. You'll need to know what the outdoor air low temperature will be and the corresponding supply water temperature you'll want to go along with that. And then the outdoor high air temperature that your boiler will still be operating at, and its corresponding supply water temperature.

For my area, Chicago, my numbers using a low temperature system might look something like this, with the outdoor air temperatures based on the Manual J heat loss load calculation:

Outdoor low air temperature - 4 degrees F
Setpoint at low air temperature - 120 degrees F
Outdoor high air temperature - 65 degrees F
Setpoint at high water temperature - 80 degrees F

These number set the Outdoor Air Reset Curve.

The tricky part is figuring out is how aggressive you want to be with the numbers? Do you set it for optimal efficiency using a 65-70 degrees indoor air temperature? That works for me but it's not up to me. It's up to those inhabiting the space and each one of those creatures has a different creature comfort zone.

There's plenty of other control settings to investigate like cascading multiple boilers, ramping, boosting, the use of a DHW indirect tank, offsets, differentials, warm weather shutdown temperatures, pump exercising, and on and on. Beware, not all boiler controls are created equal. Do your homework.

Flush condensate line.
Easy enough, right? And use an acid neutralizer kit. The condensate from these boilers is acidic and you don't want that attacking your plumbing pipes. Not to mention the fact that it's required by code in most areas.

Check static and dynamic gas pressure.
This is critical. Please don't even attempt doing a combustion analysis without first checking gas pressure while the boiler is idle (static gas pressure) and while it's operating (dynamic gas pressure). It should be, here's that phrase again, within manufacturer's specifications.

Check voltage polarity and system ground.
If your hot and neutral are crossed, you're going to have flame rectification problems.
If you have a poor ground, the flame rectification circuit will be marginalized.
Correct as needed.

Check boiler piping to verify it meets manufacturer's specifications.
This is important, as well. I wouldn't include it if it weren't.

With only a few exceptions modulating condensing boilers hold very little water, two to three gallons at best. For that reason alone. I recommend using a Low Water Cut Off on every mod con boiler. It's not an inexpensive investment. It only makes sense to protect it as best as you can.

The boilers with water tube heat exchangers are highly restrictive; the fire tube heat exchangers are more forgiving in that regard.

For these reasons, make sure you pipe them correctly ensuring proper flow through the heat exchanger. Its life depends on it. The mod cons with water tubes must be piped in some variation of primary/secondary piping whether it be closely spaced tees, a hydraulic separator, or a buffer tank. There's no way around it in my opinion. If you're not sure on the details of primary secondary piping, do whatever it takes to make sure that you are. Before long you won't even have to think about it. You'll just do it. Start with a piping schematic. Don't make it up you go along. That approach rarely ends well.

And unless you're really polished on designing hydronic piping systems, I'd recommend the same thing for boilers with fire tube heat exchangers unless they have a high water content. I can only think of two that do; one manufactured by HTP and the other by Viessmann.

You'll need to verify that you're getting the proper flow which is dictated by the manufacturer, through the heat exchanger. The numbers will tell you whether the boiler will need its own pump or not.

Check system water quality.

Would you knowingly pump contaminated gasoline into that tricked out work truck of yours? No. Who would? Then let's not put contaminated water in our high-end hydronic systems because you're going to get the same result; machinery that won't perform as God, herself, intended. No blasphemy complaints, please! I have a mom, a wife, a sister, three daughters, and two granddaughters. I recognize a power greater than myself when I see one.

We didn't pay too much attention to this in the past but with the high-end equipment, we had better start. Boiler water chemistry is more important than ever. Hardness, pH balance, TDS, and chlorine play a crucial role in the lifespan of the heat exchangers. The boiler makers will give you some ranges that you'll need to be within.

Clean your piping systems before connecting them to the new boiler and add conditioner after the new boiler is installed. Rhomar and Fernox are the brands I prefer, and I'd highly recommend either.

For additional information, please check out Caleffi idronics #18, <u>Water Quality</u>. Everything you could ever possibly want to know about water quality are within those pages.

Don't forget the usual tasks associated with a boiler clean and tune; check for gas leaks, flue pipe pitch and integrity, health & safety issues, pump maintenance, tank pressure check and adjustment, clean y-strainer, flue draft, water leaks, etc.

Testing the condensate.

Your brain, eyes, and ears are your best troubleshooting tools. Keep all of them open and your job will be easier.

Let's go to work.

CHAPTER 6 - My kind of town, Chicago is.

Wrigley Field, the Chicago Bulls who ruled the 1990's NBA, Dick Butkus, the Chicago Blackhawks winning Stanley Cups in 2010, 2013, and 2015, corrupt politicians, Union Station, diverse neighborhoods, an awesome skyline, the Belushi Brothers, Mike Royko, and boilers, boilers, and more boilers. I'm not kidding. There are boilers everywhere. This is, in fact, boiler paradise.

I'm guessing New York City may have more boilers, but I've driven in NYC. It's worse than Boston. Where do you park a service truck in Manhattan? Seriously. I can usually get from my truck to the boiler room in 100 steps or less in Chicago. Ask any service tech if that's important.

I've had the pleasure of working here my entire career and until just recently, I was getting my hands dirty, my knuckles bruised, and my head banged more times than I can remember. 0oThis is a blue-collar town if ever there was one and in the bowels of the old churches and apartments buildings, are the Kewanee, Pacific, Cleaver Brooks, and other antiquated boilers; often wrapped in brick or asbestos or a combination thereof. Many have been decommissioned, replaced, and left in the room because of the often prohibitable cost of removing them.

Those are the ones that interest me most. I no longer use the tools, but my eyes, ears, and imagination are working overtime. If only these mechanical rooms and boilers could talk? Well, they do. They always have. At least, to me they have. Everything in the mechanical room is part of the story and often plays a role in the proper functioning of the equipment. Here's one of my experiences.

Somewhere in the bowels of a church on Chicago's South Side.

Recently, I was asked to look at a Smith, 10 section, cast iron steam boiler fitted with a power burner. It was a good size apartment building on the south side of the city; the Kenwood neighborhood, I believe. The owner of the building was complaining of high gas bills going back to its installation two years ago. He hired a heating contractor to clean and tune the boiler but even after the boiler was cleaned, the CO content on the flue gas analysis was topping out at a whopping 2000 plus ppm. Wow! Right?

So, I meet the contractor out there and I asked him to check static and dynamic gas pressure. Check.

I then asked him where we're getting combustion air from. He shows me an ample sized motorized damper on the other side of the room. Check.

We start up the boiler again and ask him to break out his analyzer and insert the probe once it ramps up to high fire. I wasn't going to use my Testo 320 on a boiler that wants to kill it. Unless, of course, I had to.

Within 15 seconds or so, we're climbing northward of 2300 ppm CO. I shut the boiler off immediately to minimize risk and save his analyzer from more, unnecessary abuse.

By the way, the low-level CO sensor I wear on my belt held at 0 ppm. We're safe for now but something is wrong here. Gas pressure is rock solid and meets the burner's specifications. I double-check the free-space size of the motorized damper and we're good there too. I like to keep things simple. If we had the right amount of air and the right amount of gas, for all intents and purposes, we shouldn't be having this issue.

I'm an hour or two into this and I don't have an answer yet, but I'm not discouraged. Like I said, I like challenges. It's just an air/gas ratio thing. The boiler is a big one, but the principle is the same. We have too much of one, gas; and not enough of the other, air. How hard can it be?

The gas pressure is spot on and the air is more than sufficient. The only thing that can cause it to overfire now is the wrong orifice, or no orifice. It can't be that. Right?

That's when I get the best idea I've had in a long time. I call a guy who has more experience at this than I do. There's not much he hasn't seen. If you say you don't know anyone smarter than yourself, you might be surrounding yourself with the wrong people. I tell my pal and mentor what's going on and he agrees that we've taken all the right steps so far and we're being as thorough as one could be. He's proud. He's taught me a lot through the years. And then, this.

My pal: Have you checked the orifice?

Me: I thought of that but haven't done it yet.

My pal: Well, why not?

Me: It can't be the orifice? Can it? Ya think I should check it?

My pal: Yes, I think you should check it. Why else would I bring it up?

Me: Ok. It's easy enough to do on this power burner so I'll give it a look.

My pal: That'd be great.

It really is easy, probably easier than checking an orifice on a residential boiler. On the gas train, there's a 2" plug on the run of a 2" tee that you spin off and the orifice will be staring you right in the face. As soon as I shine my flashlight light on it, I'm 99.9% certain this was the problem. Curl your index finger over until its tip hits the tip of your thumb. That's roughly the size of the orifice I was looking at.

That's a very large orifice.

I pulled it out, called the number into the factory, and it turns out the installing company used an orifice that was about twice the size that it should have been. They obviously never did a combustion analysis at start-up. The manufacturer ships the properly sized orifice overnight and it goes in as easily as the old one came out. We start the boiler up and I use my analyzer to see how the numbers are doing. Just as sure as my pal is smarter than me, the combustion numbers look better than a Jon Lester fist bump after going 7 strong innings. Again.

All in all, I'd call it a win. We solved a large, unusual problem the first time out. We, being the operative word. I also was reminded that I should have acted on my hunch. Don't be afraid to pick up the phone to ask a colleague a question or to bounce something off them. Sometimes the best thing to know is the right number to call. It's not about having all the answers but rather knowing where to find them.

CHAPTER 7 – Fire & Flow

These two words are part and parcel to the proper design, installation, and troubleshooting in the world of hot water space heating.

If we have too much of one, too little of the other, none of either, or any combination thereof, your phone is going to light up like a Caleffi Zone Valve Relay in January.

And when we're in the bowels of buildings figuring stuff out, we don't have the time to be reading run-on paragraphs so I'm going to hit the necessary facts with bullet points. I like to keep things simple and straight-forward. Flow is where we're going to start.

Qualifying or Selecting a Circulator
- Start with a **Manual J Heat Loss Calculation.** You can't size a pump properly without knowing how much heat you need to move so start here, always. If the building has only one zone with one pump, you'll use the heat loss for the entire building. If there's multiple zones, you'll need a heat loss requirement for each zone and size the pumps accordingly.
- The next step is to establish a **Target Flow Rate** in gallons per minute, GPM, using the following formula:
  GPM = BTU/h Loss/(500 x Delta T)
- The **Delta T** is the number we use in our design to establish the temperature difference between supply water temperature and return water temperature. And that number is going to change based on the application. 10 degrees F is typically used for **residential radiant heating,** 20 degrees F **for commercial radiant heating,** 20 degrees F for high temperature applications such as those using **radiators or baseboard. Snow and ice melt systems** will get you up to 25 degrees F Delta T.
- Our **Pipe Size** is based on GPM with flow velocities between 2-4 per second. Why 2-4 per second? That's a very good question! I could give you an answer that would involve mathematical formulas, but I'll leave that for guys a lot smarter than I am. John Siegenthaler's name immediately comes to mind.
  Here's the long and short of it – if the water is moving too slow, the air bubbles in the water will not be able to move along horizontal pipe and cause all kinds of problems for you. Specifically, we won't get those air bubbles back to our air separator where they can be expelled from the system. If it's moving too fast, you're going to have noise issues and potentially pipe erosion.
- This next step can be as tricky, or as simple, as you want it to be. We must find the **Head Loss** or **Feet of Head** of the piping system. The easiest way for me to explain this is *anything* that causes resistance to our water flow, GPM, is part of the Head Loss. A tee, a 90 degrees elbow, a flow check, y-strainer, ball valve, length of pipe, and many other components are all part of this equation. Each will have a

value assigned to it called its **Equivalent Length of Pipe** based on its description and size. Basically, you add up all the values and plug them into a pesky little equation that looks like this:

Hl = k x c x l x (f1.75 power)
Hl = the head of the piping system
k = value based on the pipe size
c = correction factor for something being used other than water and its temperature
l = total equivalent length of the piping circuit
f1.75 = flow rate raised to 1.75 power

Ughhh! I hear ya! I apologize for dumping that on you. Seriously, the last thing I want you to do is start daydreaming. I want you engaged. Reading that mess certainly did not spark enthusiasm in your desire to continue. But stay with me here.

The fact is this method is almost impossible when you're troubleshooting. Unless, of course, there are exposed walls and ceilings throughout the building which would allow you to count and itemize every fitting, measure every length of pipe, find the TEL (total equivalent length) of every other component, plug them into the equation, and do the math.

That has happened exactly ZERO times in my career. So, lets thank the smart people again for making this easier on all of us who have a schedule to keep and continue to struggle for the legal tender. Those same smart people came up with an insanely easy way to arrive at a number for head loss that any third grader who pays attention could solve. Here goes –

- Measure the number of feet of the longest run of pipe to and from the pump. This will take an assumption or two on your part, but it will get us relatively close.
- Multiply this number by 1.5.
- Multiply that number by .04.
- That's it! That final number is our **Pump Head**, or the Head Loss.

Is it as accurate as the first option? No, of course not. How could it be? In the first option we're dealing concrete data based on real numbers and actual measurements. We had access to the entire system.

But we're solving problems in a 50 year old home under conditions that we deal with as is. And "as is" often involves a customer that wants answers and solutions sooner than later. The latter option will keep those customers happy *and* get you the correct replacement pump at the same time. Ignorant is not a good look and you'll never have to worry about that with this plan of attack.

- Our final step is selecting a circulator based on the Pump GPM and the Pump Head. These two numbers make up our last Bold Red Term I'm going to use, the **Target Operating Point.**
- The Target Operating Point gives a specific place to plot our needs on a graph of your favorite circulator manufacturer's pump curves and see which pump best fits your application.
- We're looking for a pump curve that passes through our Target Operating Point or the one that is directly above it.

- This point should fall within the middle third flow rate range of the pump curve for maximum efficiency.

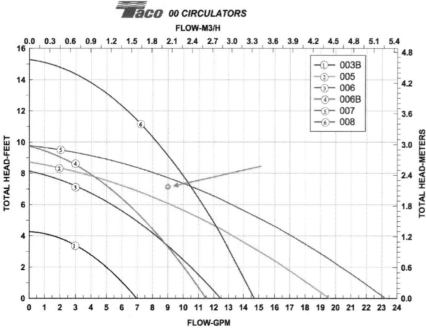

Taco 00 CIRCULATORS

FLOW-M3/H

Legend:
- ①— 003B
- ②— 005
- ③— 006
- ④— 006B
- ⑤— 007
- ⑥— 008

Courtesy of Taco Comfort.

- In this case, my choice would be number 5, the 007, because it meets all the criteria above.

Let's take a quick look at an existing pump selection and size. We have an average size, 2 story home in the northwest suburbs of Chicago. The heating system is an older 80,000 BTU/h cast iron boiler serving cast iron baseboard, piped reverse return, throughout the home. They called you because they're having trouble heating one bedroom that has a single length of baseboard in it. In fact, the baseboard is ice cold.

They already tried another company but didn't have faith in them because they were told the existing Taco pump wasn't big enough and they needed something with more power; his words, not mine. The other guy wasn't even there long enough to take off his jacket.

So, you arrive at the scene and break out your tools, a pad of paper, a pencil, and your iPhone's calculator.

Customer says, "What are you doing?

"I'm double checking to see if your Taco 007 pump is big enough. It will only take a couple of minutes."

Customer "Well I guess if it's only going take a couple of minutes that'll be alright, but I've never seen a service tech operate like this before."

Let's see-

We have an 80,000 BTU/h boiler using cast iron baseboard, so we'll be figuring a 20 degrees Delta T.

80,000/(500 x 20) = 80,000/10,000 = **8 GPM**

After some quick measurements, you find that the longest length of pipe comes to around 140 feet.

140 x 1.5 = 210' Total Equivalent Length accounting for the fittings and pipe size

210 x .04 = **8.4' Head Loss**

8 GPM @ 8.4' Head Loss

"I got it."

Customer – "You've got what?"

"I know if you're pump is the right size."

Customer – "Well, is it?"

"It sure is."

Customer – "You're certain of that? It only took you a couple of minutes."

"I'm absolutely certain. You need a pump that will deliver 8 GPM @ 8.4' Pump Head and your Taco 007 is fully capable of doing that."

Customer – "Well, I don't know exactly what all that means and what the heck was that other guy trying to sell me? A bag of goods?"

"No sir. He was trying to sell you a pump that you didn't need."

Customer – "Ok, that's just fine and dandy but our bedroom is still pretty dang cold, ya know."

"Yes sir. Considering the way your system is piped and that being the only room that's cold, I'm betting it's a frozen pipe or just an air-bound length of baseboard. I'll check for air first. That's only going to take a minute or two as well."

Lucky for the customer in this fictional story, it was just air.

And, also lucky for this customer he called a qualified company the second time around. The tech didn't get the pump sale this time, but I bet he got a customer for life. If, you know, it was a real story and all.

I've mentioned it before. Don't be the ripping and running type of contractor or technician. Learn your craft as well as you possibly can and utilize that knowledge to grow your career or your business. The dishonest and unqualified ones are a dime a dozen and easy to spot.

For further information and help, I've added these notes, tools, and chart.

Helpful Notes:
- When zone valves are used, use a flat curve pump or a delta P pump to account for the valves opening and closing; otherwise, you're going to be adding a bypass pressure differential valve.
- Use integrated pump check valves wherever possible because they are less restrictive than weighted check valves; less restriction, less head loss.
- Also, consider a larger pipe size if it falls within recommended velocities over a smaller pipe so a smaller pump can be considered.
- Pumps in Series – Head doubles, GPM stays the same.
- Pumps in Parallel – Head stays the same, GPM doubles.

Helpful Tools:
- B&G System Syzer Calculator Wheel
- B&G System Syzer Software
- Siegenthaler's Hydronic Design Suite
- Siegenthaler's Modern Hydronic Heating textbook, 3rd edition
- Caleffi's idronics Issue 16
- Taco Technical Documents 9 and 10.

Thanks Gil!

The second critical ingredient is Fire and we've all had our run-ins with that, I suppose.

Early on, I had my eyebrows scorched from a late light off. Now, I always have one hand on the disconnect switch when I'm firing one up that may have delayed ignition.

I've seen RTU panels blown across a roof from delayed ignition.

I've seen a burner mounted sideways, and firing, on a manifold. That's how fires start.

I've seen a hole in a heat exchanger so big I could put my fist through. And this was one day after another company did maintenance on it. All I had to do was pull the rollout shield. It was right there and impossible to miss.

I've seen a steam boiler side panel glowing cherry red.

I've seen flame rollout so bad that every wire in the boiler vestibule was burnt to a crisp.

I've seen every limit switch, rollout switch, and fusible link known to man jumped out. Don't do that. Ever.

I've cleaned enough soot filled boilers and furnaces that I'm perfectly content to never clean one again. And unless it's my own equipment, I won't.

The moment I walk into a boiler room my eyes and ears and nose are on high alert.

If the burner(s) is lighting rough, I want to hear it.

If the flame is rolling out, I want to see it.

If something is burning slightly, I want to smell it.

And If I smell natural gas and something slightly burning at the same time, I'm reaching for the service disconnect switch and gas shutoff right now.

Don't discount some of your most valuable tools, your eyes, ears, and nose. The more experience you add to your resume', the better tuned your senses become.

Yes, the customer is likely to be shadowing you and telling you how he has been timing the gaps between the loud booms for the past 23 1/2 hours and that information is important, but you have to be a selective listener to a degree. Listen for the key words and lock in on them.

At first, you need to focus on what you're seeing, hearing, and smelling. After that, it's time to break out the tools and test instruments. And if you're anything like me, this is what it's all about anyway. We love using our tools and we love buying them more. It's the best part of the job after depositing the checks; using the JB gas pressure gauge, Testo 320 analyzer, digital thermometers, UEI gas sniffer, Fluke multimeter, and the assortment of Klein, Wera, Knipex, Gear Wrench, Craftsman, Wiha, and Stanley hand tools is why we're doing this, right? Right! We can justify the purchase of almost any tool on planet Earth to our significant others as being part and parcel to us being the incredible technicians we are. So, if we're going to buy them, let's use them.

I like to address the things that are blatantly wrong right off the bat. Pull and clean the burners, make sure the burners are aligned correctly, repair burned wiring and secure them away from the heat, make sure the rollout shield is secured in place, check for and fix gas leaks, look for signs of flue gas spillage, check integrity and pitch of flue pipe.

Many of these things would fall under the category of "checklist" type items. The rubber really doesn't hit the road until we start using the test instruments, recording values, and adjusting if needed. This is usually what separates the heavyweight techs from the rip and run crews.

And that difference can be boiled to just a few things – knowledge, the desire for more knowledge, personal integrity, and taking pride in a job done well.

I'm going to hit on some of the most important things to know by way of one of my favorite tools, the bullet point. It's not like I'm making a mixed tape for you. I just want you to get the goods in one in a clear, concise way. Here goes.

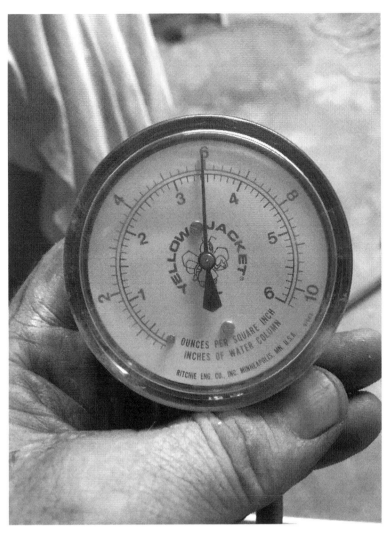

Incoming gas pressure.

Typical Troubleshooting and Maintenance Testing

- Verifying voltage and polarity.
- Gas Pressure – This step is critical for so many reasons and check with the manufacturer specifications if you don't know what they require. Sometimes the required gas pressure is higher than you might think; some gas-fired infrared heaters come to mind as an example.
- Combustion Analysis – Safety, compliance, consistency, and efficiency are some solid reasons to do it. This will give an accurate representation of how your burner is firing. Tune it, if necessary, to the manufacturer's recommendations. Leave a copy of the printed results with your customer.
- Clocking the Gas Meter
    1. Turn off all appliances except for the one you're testing.
    2. Make sure the one you're checking is firing.
    3. For residential work, the 1/2 cubic feet gas dial works fine. This means for every revolution, **.5 cubic feet** of gas is being burned.

4. Time the dial for exactly one minute, **60 seconds** and count the number of revolutions in that one minute.

5. Look at this example:

2.2 revolutions in one minute

2.2 X **.5** = 1.1 cubic feet/minute

1.1 X **60** = 66 cubic feet of gas

66 x **1038** = **68,508 BTU/h Input**

*1038 equals the BTU/h/cubic ft. as verified on my gas bill.

Properties of Gas

- Unlike LP gas, it's lighter than air. The engineers assign a value to that called Specific Gravity. Air has a Specific Gravity of 1.0. How convenient! Anything less than 1.0 is lighter than air. Anything greater than 1.0 is heavier than air.
- The Specific Gravity of Natural Gas is 0.60, and lighter than air.
- The Specific Gravity of Propane Gas is about 1.5, and heavier than air.
- The heat content of Natural Gas ranges from 950-1125 BTU/h per cubic foot. An estimation of 1000 BTU/h cubic foot will get you close. For precise numbers, check with your utility or your utility bill to confirm exactly what yours is.
- The heat content of Propane Gas is approximately 2500 BTU/h per cubic foot.
- Natural Gas ignites between 1100 - 1200 degrees F.
- Propane Gas ignites between 920 - 1020 degrees F.
- Both are extremely dangerous, but propane is more likely to linger because of its weight (Specific Gravity) and lights off quicker.

So Many Efficiencies

- Combustion Efficiency – The ability of the boiler to convert fuel to heat energy. It's based on a theoretical heat value because as I mentioned above that value varies based on your local utility.
- Steady State Efficiency – Combustion efficiency when the flue gas temperature has stabilized (stopped rising) and the flue gas samples level off.
- Annual Fuel Utilization Efficiency – This is the one we use to sell equipment, but it won't be accurate with a poorly designed system. It's a seasonal average, expressed in percentages, required by the Federal Trade Commission. It considers the cycling losses, chimney losses, and jacket losses.
- Thermal Efficiency – The rate at which the heat exchanger transfers heat to the medium, usually water or air.

There is an infinite amount of information that can be learned regarding the servicing and troubleshooting of gas-fired burners. There are entire chapters and entire books dedicated to these topics. I'm going touch on a few of the problems you may encounter during service schedule on any given day.

Burner Problems

- Overfired – Check gas pressure, firing rate, and Delta T. This can lead to short cycling, early control, equipment failure, soot, inefficiency, and a host of other issues.
- Underfired – Check gas pressure, firing rate, and Delta T. Some of the symptoms would be inadequate heat, flue gas condensation which isn't good for a lot equipment, inefficiency, and shortened equipment life.
- Delayed Ignition – This can be caused by dirty burners, dirty burner crossovers, low gas pressure, and misaligned burners.
- Floating Flame & Flame Rollout – Most of the time this is caused by plugged up boiler sections/heat exchanger, a crack or hole in the heat exchanger. Soot, too little secondary air, and an improper burn are usually the culprits.
- Yellow Tipping – This is caused by flame impingement or incomplete combustion; the latter being too much gas or too little primary air.
- Lifting Flame – Just as it says, the flame is literally lifting above the burner. Too much primary is the cause.

There's More…

- *Be aware.* Make sure the boiler room has a properly sized air source for combustion. In commercial rooms, my preference is always a motorized damper with an end switch.
- *Don't assume.* I've had two different jobs in the past year where the cause of the problem was grossly oversized orifices on commercial power burners.
- *Don't ever* jump out any type of safety control and walk away from the equipment. There's never a good enough reason to put property or people in harm's way.
- *Be through.* Nobody likes callbacks especially your boss, supervisor, and customer.

And Finally,

- *Be safe.* My singed eyebrows recovered but that could have, and should have, been avoided. Think it through, double check your work, and verify with testing not guessing. And wear a Low Level CO Sensor on your person when you're on the job.

We've got a problem here.

CHAPTER 8 – Steam Efficiency

Why aren't we trying harder to make steam heating systems more efficient? It seems to me we can reduce the size of most steam boilers and, at the same time, reduce their carbon footprint. I've had this idea rolling around in my for about 4 months. At first, I thought I was on to some revolutionary idea but I should have known better. Take a look.

My favorite radiator.

I know that we size steam boilers by EDR and we size hot water boilers by the heat loss of the building.

But, if we're being energy conscious, why not do the following for a steam system design and steam boiler replacements?

• Perform a heat loss calculation on the building.
• Perform an EDR calculation on the radiation.
• Let's assume for now that the EDR outweighs the heat loss significantly. It usually does.
• Remove or resize radiators, *or better yet install orifices on the radiators*, to match the room by room heat loss of each room.
• Size the new steam boiler to reflect the new EDR that we now have.

Turns out, this proposition has been around longer than I have, but why hasn't it been implemented more?

To me, this makes perfect sense. I know there's a considerable amount of work involved but for large multifamily buildings the fuel savings must be significant. To get a better understanding, I turned to the Steam Pros at www.heatinghelp.com. And with permission from Erin Holohan, HeatingHelp's President, I'm sharing some of that conversation.

Steam Pro: Isn't someone running a well-'undersized' system (closely matching the heat loss, not the EDR) with good results?

Me: For the most part, I'm suggesting the same thing here but on a much larger scale. Hundreds of large multifamily buildings heated with steam in Chicago.

Steam Pro: I also have given this some consideration. If there is 1/3 more connected EDR than needed to heat the building, could we just ignore the last 1/3 of the radiator? Isn't that cooler 1/3 just then part of the return piping, especially in a 2-pipe system. In a 1- pipe wouldn't the steam only travel the hot 2/3 and then the thermostat hopefully shuts down the system? Maybe I am being too simplistic in this thought process. However, this summer I installed orifices in a 2-pipe system, sized to heat only 60-80% of the EDR of each radiator. This is in an old school house that has had major window upgrades or removal. This is the coldest winter we have had in many years, if kids and teachers were cold I would have been made aware of it.

Me: That's encouraging! Here's some more information -Again, large buildings with large boilers; 750 MBH to 4000 MBH. Hundreds of them so the potential savings would be epic. Industrial Combustion modulating burners with tight control, 1.2 psi max. Also, I have no skin in the game. I'm not a contractor anymore. I work for a well-established, non-profit company in Chicago. We facilitate and provide oversight for projects such as lighting upgrades, air sealing, insulation, HVAC, and smaller measures as well. I'm just trying to get the gas and electrical meters to spin slower and a way to quantify the savings.

Steam Pro: 90% of the boilers are oversized due to new envelope upgrades and removal of radiation. Also, if not that then there is simply usually too much radiation in the original design. Maybe not if you leave the windows to comply with the 1918 pandemic. But everyone (except me) gets a flu shot so that is no longer a worry. I did ask Dan Holohan at a seminar in the Twin Cities if radiators were orifice controlled to 80%, then could the boiler be sized to 80% less than the connected EDR. He replied that, yes, it could be done.

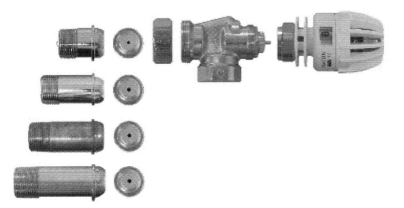

TRV orifices.

Me: *Yes, this is what I was looking for!*

Steam Pro: *As the least experienced and least knowledgeable person on this thread, I am going to chime in. I am replacing most of the radiators in my house (for reasons more to do with design aesthetic and less to do with efficiency), and I purchased the replacements based on heat loss calculations because I thought that was how you were supposed to do it. (Is that not how people do it?) Steve, to put real numbers to your hypothetical:*

1. *Perform a heat loss calculation: Mine came out to about 44,000 BTU/hr.*
2. *Perform an EDR Calculation on the radiation. Current radiators: 75,000 BTU/hr.*
3. *Removed or reside radiators to match the room by room heat loss: I built in a fudge factor so the new radiation totals 50,000 BTU/hr.*
4. *Size the new steam boiler to reflect the new EDR: So... my current boiler is a Weil-McLain EG/PEG-50 (or 55... I never bothered to count the burners) kicking out 145,000 or 167,000 BTU/hr. It's running just fine, but when it finally kicks the bucket, I was planning on replacing it with a much smaller one. I was surprised that the boiler is so oversized relative to the existing radiation. By a factor of 2, is that industry standard?*

Me: *You sound very knowledgeable to me. Experience can be overrated at times. You're running on the same track I am, and I like it.*

Steam Pro: *I know two guys that have written on the possibilities of downsizing steam systems. They focused on using inlet orifices in two-pipe radiators. They pointed out that since the orifices separate the radiators from the boiler and mains, the pickup factor is not needed. Also, by adjusting orifice capacities it is possible to downsize radiators that may have been erroneously oversized, bringing the system into balance. Also, since pickup factor is not a part of the equation, this means that the boiler can indeed be sized for the building loss as opposed to the connected radiation. Similar gains by downsizing one-pipe systems may be possible, but it is a more delicate balancing act. A few years ago, I helped a friend straighten out a Moline system in his house that was a disaster. The guts of the moline valves had been removed and so it was a two-pipe system with no traps and an oversized boiler made it worse. We installed inlet orifices on all the radiators. The boiler started leaking about the same time, so the Weil McLain EGH-12 with an input of 550,000 BTU was replaced with an EGH-75, with an input of 299,000 BTU. The system has connected radiation of 1197 and the new boiler had an EDR rating of only 750 sq. ft. But there is more to consider when connecting a boiler to orifice systems such as a Moline, or any other similar system. First, since the radiator is separated from the mains and the boiler by an orifice, it never sees pressure. Not even the 6-8 oz. that is in the mains. So, instead of 240 BTU/sq. ft., it's more like 225 BTU/sq. ft. Then, you leave out the pickup allowance. If you keep the piping loss allowance, it's 15%. But, if the mains and risers to the upper floors are insulated, and if the system is oversized, you can leave that off too. In addition, we made the conservative decision* to size the new boiler at 90% of the radiator capacity, with zero allowances. That brought down to needing a boiler capable of outputting 242,530 BTU. The EGH-75 has a DOE output of 247,000. How does it work? Like a charm. They are silent except a rare clank from expansion of one radiator. On a prolonged firing, coming out of a setback, the radiators feel fully heated to the touch. But no steam ever gets into the returns. The sound of steam going through the orifices is barely audible. Overall, the heat is even. All radiators heat uniformly steam distribution is even throughout the entire system. Operating cost has gone down significantly (I don't have the numbers) and the cost of the replacement boiler was significantly lower than a conventionally matched boiler.

Me: I knew I came to the right place. Thanks again, Erin! This is beginning to sound like science and empirical evidence.

Steam Pro: The Moline system was also my inspiration for using supply valve orifice plates in two pipe steam systems. We have several homes and multi-unit buildings that we've done over the past 10 years and those system work exceptionally well. On two pipe systems we always look at the historic fuel usage and with some educated guesses on the heating plant efficiency, work out the actual heat loss of the structure. For two pipe systems installed before WWII, the typical radiation capacity calculates out to be about 60% higher than needed for design conditions and this is assuming that the piping is making no heat contribution to the structure.

When we size the orifices, we typically size them to this number. Back in the boiler room, we either down-fire the existing boiler or if replacing, install a much smaller boiler that is sized to this new radiation loss plus a 15% pick up factor. This process still has a lot of built in extra capacity (the contribution of the pipes heating the building, for instance), but results in a heating plant usually about 1/3 to 1/2 the capacity of the existing or less. This process has also allowed us to do many other things that normally are not possible. One big one is to eliminate the need for a vacuum pump on larger systems. Since Vacuum system piping is about 1/2 the capacity of pressure systems and we are now running about 1/2 the steam to feed the system, the new piping is now the optimum size for the new system capacity. This assumes you have no lifts in the system. When possible, we couple an orifice system with an outdoor reset boiler control that modulates the burner based on outdoor temp.

We currently have these running two ways, one system is resetting the burner output based on the outdoor temperature while the other is modulating the target pressure in the system based on outdoor temperature. Out of the two, the first is probably the best choice due to the nature of flow through an orifice. Orifices flow a very large amount of steam at very low pressure differences, so as the pressure is increased across the orifices as the outdoor temperature drops, the increase in heating is relatively small. The results of these change naturally mimic those of a hot water system upgraded to a modulating heat source with outdoor reset. Very stable and even heating throughout the structure and extremely quiet operation. Even with systems of questionable piping (some sags in steam mains or radiator runouts) noise is nearly eliminated since the piping almost never cools to allow water hammer to occur. Expansion noises also disappear.

And of course, there are fuel savings, despite areas that were previously too cold are now heated. While most of the systems we have worked on have had multiple changes made at the same time as the installation of orifices, the analysis of the first seasons fuel usage was a reduction of about 40%.

Reducing the firing rate below radiation capacity is more of a chance on a one pipe steam, especially in multi-unit *buildings since people will tinker with the radiator vents, eventually throwing the system out of balance. In a single-family home, however, it seems to work.*

Me: *That's a big help. Thank you! How would I know which size orifice to use?*

Steam Pro: *I have used Tunstall's cup type orifice plates. I size them from their table, which shows the range of EDR at various pressures. I have always used the 0.5 PSI (8oz). When doing a Moline system, which were intended to operate on 6 oz, I choose the next larger orifice if it's at the upper end of the range on the chart.*

My own system controls with a 2-stage burner between the pressures of 7-11oz. Since I have working traps I don't know if I would be passing any steam into the returns, but I doubt it. On the Moline system, they work just great. Or course, the obvious thing is, sizing the boiler to maintain the pressure within the parameters of the orifice sizing is key.

Me: *This is sounding better and better. Anyone else?*

Steam Pro: *It depends on the system and how it will be operated. If we are trying to retain or convert to a gravity return, we will size to 1/2 psi drop so we will have plenty of stacking height on the radiator return main drops. If we are planning on running outdoor reset of the steam pressure, we design for a 3 PSI pressure drop. Tunstall recommends 4 psi, but 3 seem to work fine and that's what we have charts for. The only complaint we have seen is there is a slight whistling when running at high pressures through the 3 psi orifices. With a properly sized on/off boiler or with outdoor reset, this won't happen very often. We size the orifices based on the radiation capacity and the heat loss of the structure. We usually find that we can met the heat loss on the design day with the radiators only 60% filled, so that ends up being our design load for the system and we size the boiler accordingly. We only had one system that ran a bit short on capacity during our -20F days a month or so ago, so we know we are hitting our target well because design day is only -4F. The new replacement boilers installed with the new orifices are usually about 2/5 to 1/2 the capacity of the previous boiler. I have been using a 15% pick up factor for sizing the boilers, not the 33% since the orifices reduce the start-up load dramatically from the studies I've read. I believe one guy, in New York, has also been using a 15% pick up factor for quite some time.*

Me: *How, specifically, are we saving energy by properly sizing a steam boiler?*

Steam Pro: *Attached is an efficiency curve that is often referenced if using atmospheric boilers with no stack damper. I have found it quite accurate for predicting fuel savings when reducing boiler capacity to proper levels. Oversized atmospheric boilers on steam systems can be particularly inefficient because the radiators installed in most buildings between 1900 and 1940 are also about 60% oversized for the heating load.*

The typical steam boiler sized to radiation with a standard 33% pick up factor will have about twice the capacity necessary to heat a building on the coldest day. If your boiler is 2.25 times the size required for the radiators, you may be about 4.5 times oversized for the heat load. This would yield a seasonal efficiency around 52%, assuming a steady state efficiency around 78% (which is realistic number for most modern atmospheric steam boiler). A stack damper may help this number some under the right conditions.

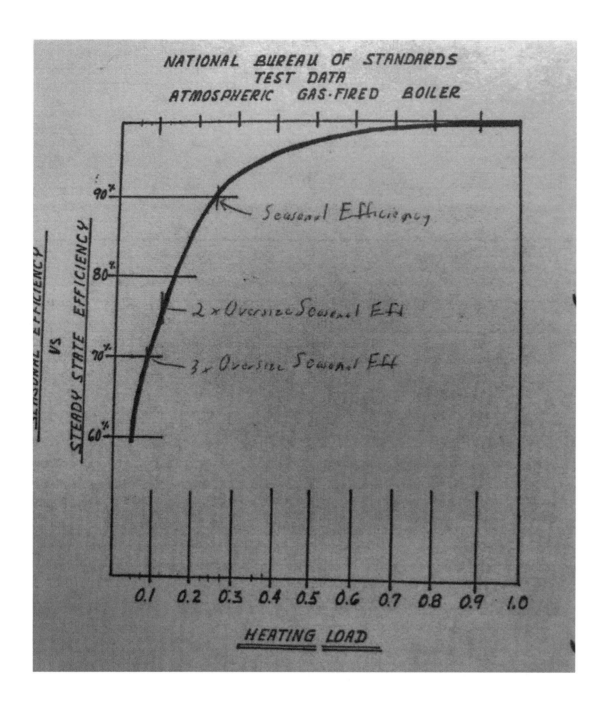

Those are some impressive numbers reflecting the potential savings. I think, as an industry, we should give more consideration to make steam systems as energy efficient as we can. We owe it to the building owners, ourselves, and our environment. I'd like to add the use of radiator orifices as a means of reducing boiler size as one of our measures.

Thanks again to Erin Holohan and the Steam Pros who contributed to this idea.

Heatinghelp.com, the place where steam problems go to die, and ideas come alive.

C H A P T E R 9 – Boiler Room Prefabrication

The way I see it, we have three ways to put together a boiler room. We can piece it together on site, fitting by fitting, following a piping schematic. We can buy a prefabricated panel from a manufacturer. Or we can build our own prefab panel suited specifically for the job it's intended for. I've done it every which way to Sunday. For me, prefabbing my own is the best way and one of the things I enjoyed most as a contractor. For the past 15 years, it's been an easy choice for me.

It's not like having to choose between Willie, Mickey, and the Duke; three guys who played the same position, in the same sport, in the same city, at the same time, and all three enshrined in the Baseball Hall of Fame. Willie Mays, Mickey Mantle, and Duke Snider all played center field In New York City in the 1950's. Willie roamed the Polo Grounds for the Giants in Upper Manhattan, Duke manned Ebbets Field in Brooklyn for the real Dodgers, and Mickey succeeded Joe DiMaggio at Yankee Stadium in the Bronx. How do you choose between those three guys? Who's the best? The New York fan base had it a lot tougher than us boiler guys do.

For me, at least, the decision to prefab my own is a no-brainer. The concept has been around for a long time. Wirsbo and Danfoss were making panels decades ago. I started making my own in the early 2000's. Some contractors, like me, swear by it while others say they just don't have time for it; the latter point I hope to convince you is just flat out wrong.

I'm going to show you why it's the best way and how I did it and why I loved doing it and why I miss it.

The job is sold, the design is complete, and you've got your down payment. Now is the time when the customer's expectations are at their highest so far in the process. They've picked your company over two other reputable competitors. They've trusted you with their money to get things moving in the right direction for their hydronic system that has been problematic for years. It's time for you to deliver now on your promises and guarantees. No going back now.

Measuring the Job

I start with my initial piping schematic. This way, I have an idea how much wall space I'm going to need. There's going to be times where it just doesn't seem possible that a prefab panel will work or fit. I'm urging you to be creative and think outside the box before giving up. Take this mess for example.

I have a limited amount of space to work with. Just to the right of the boiler, there's the return drop for the AC air handler. On the left, I'm being jammed by the electrical box. The back wall isn't doing me any favors either. There's gas pipe, 4 sticks of 1/2" EMT, and a backflow preventor for their swimming pool.

I'm committed to making this new system look as good as it will work. After giving this a lot of thought and review, I'm ready to share my plan with the owners. The extra hour of imaginative thinking is going to save me ten times that amount of time in execution. It's kind of like the "measure twice, cut once" theory.

Here's my plan:

- I have 64" of back wall to work with and an almost unlimited amount of height if I remove the aforementioned gas, electric, and backflow preventor.
- I'll swing the new boiler 90 degrees to the left making the entire back wall a blank canvas. The right -hand side of the Lochinvar Knight will not extend any further into the room than the existing Dunkirk; a win-win.

- Every hydronic pipe and component in the picture will be removed and replaced by someone not named Moe, Larry, and Curly.
- A bit more detail – the existing boiler is serving 6 bathrooms with radiant floors, two detached garages, and one relatively small snowmelt zone. Each bathroom is on its own zone and I plan to change that to a single zone controlled by the Master Bathroom thermostat. This will prevent the inevitable short cycling that's been occurring.
- I'm also going to move all the snowmelt components to an adjacent unused closet, glycol throughout.

It doesn't happen all the time, but the owners were very forward-thinking people and gave me the go ahead on everything I suggested.

Back at the Shop

I tweak my drawing to meet the challenges and arrangement of the room. On my largest bench, I roll out some blue masking exactly 64" apart. Within those 64", I'm going to build a new a new boiler room.

In the shop, I have all the fittings, pipes, pumps, zone valves, isolation valves, relays, lengths of strut, strut clamps, plywood, paint, tools, ball valves, torches, solder, press tools, threading tools, electrical supplies etc. that I could possibly need. All of them neatly arranged and organized near the benches for the sole purpose of efficient prefabrication.

I also can play whatever music I want and as loud as I want. I don't have to take my Red Wings on and off all day long running back and forth to the truck for this, that, the other thing, and the thing I forgot the last trip to the truck. I don't have to ask to use the washroom throughout the day. There's not a tarp laid out anywhere. Why would there be? It's a shop floor. Oh, and maybe I'll order a sausage, pepper, and onion pizza for lunch? You see where I'm going with this? For Boiler Guys and Gals, this is a small piece of Heaven. I am truly in my element and once I get rolling, I'm not leaving till it's done. That's how much I enjoy doing this stuff. If it wasn't my job, it would've been my hobby. 7-8 hours later and it's going to look like this.

Prefab on the shop bench.

Do you see how I've used the strut and clamps to lock in my pipe by attaching it to the bench? I don't want the new black panel getting all messed up, so I wait until the piping is complete before transferring over to the actual panel. It's the little things that add up to big differences.

Don't forget the electric and control wiring. A lot of that can be done in the shop too. If you're not pre-wiring after you pre-pipe, you're leaving money on the table. Don't leave money on the table.

Painted and pressure tested.

Once I'm done piping, I slide my work onto a precut, pre-painted piece of 3/4" plywood. From there, I wire the circulators, relays, zone valves, mixing valves, and transformers as far as I can. I'll even add a 1900 box and service switch. The placement of the boiler supply and return on the bottom of right of the picture was no accident. You want to get everything lined up as best you can so that when you get on site, everything falls into place.

I've gone as big as 4' x 8' panels without having a problem of getting them on my Chevy Express 250 cargo van.

And Back to the Job

This is the time and place where you can expect the word "WOW!" When you take their boiler room from the top picture to this picture, they're going to be impressed. I guarantee it.

Back on the site and moving forward.

And you've saved a ton of money and effort and had fun doing it. There were 15 exterior concrete stairs leading to the basement of this home. But the boiler room was all the way on the other side of the basement and that path was covered with expensive carpet. I saved myself so much time and energy by thinking this one all the way through, coming up with a detailed plan, and then executing the plan.

By the way, I think Willie Mays was the greatest baseball player who ever lived. I think Mickey Mantle could have been if it weren't for injuries and some other things. Duke Snider played for my favorite baseball team not from Chicago. Honestly, any one of these guys would be a choice.

Choose wisely when piping your boiler rooms.

CHAPTER 10 – Sales, A Different Approach

Never have I asked for the sale when on a sales call. Not once, ever. What!? Yup, it's true. I was always confident enough that I'd have a good shot at getting the job without having to ask. Promoting your business is good but having people attracted to it makes the sale so much more satisfying, and easier. And asking for the sale is putting pressure on your potential customer when it's not necessary. They may have another contractor due to stop by an hour after you leave and they're almost always going to run this by someone else before a decision is made. Why make them feel uncomfortable?

Hang on...being told I'm not supposed to say things like that. Oh well. I did. And I'm not apologizing. And I'm certain the professional sales managers and salespeople who read this will think I'm stoned, drunk, or just plain uninformed. That's ok and I can assure you I'm none of the above. I'm telling you what worked for me for a long time. And it may work for you too. You do you. That's a popular saying now, right? Not bad advice if you ask me.

I respect people who work in sales, but I wouldn't want their jobs. They have sales quotas and monthly sales meetings where their dismal numbers are displayed in front of all the sales superstars. Some of my best friends are salespeople and when they go from job to job, they're often required to learn an entirely different industry and product line. I want to buy from someone that is knowledgeable with vast experience in the goods and products that I wish to purchase.

So, what exactly did I do on a sales call? Great question.

First off, I actively listened to every word they said. I wasn't thinking about any sales pitch or how I'm going to dazzle them with my brilliance. I wanted to know what they wanted. The easiest way to lose someone is by not paying close attention or interrupting them before they've expressed their concerns and their desired outcome. Listen, listen, and listen. Successful sales, in my opinion, is listening more than you talk.

Rarely, has someone asked for something that was completely unreasonable and if they did, I would respectfully and gently offer them a better plan of attack. I had one customer who insisted that I install isolation valves on his refrigerant lines before the evaporator coil so he could pull and clean the coil annually. A competitor told him the day before that this would be a great way to accomplish that goal. I assured him it wasn't and then explained how easy it is to access the underside of a cased coil without removing the coil and all the associated work that comes with that. I think that sale was made right then and there.

My sales technique was to always be better prepared than my competitor, not be the slickest. My method of operation was to gather all the necessary information by taking notes and lots of pictures. Pictures are invaluable for the purposes of putting together a bid. I'd let the owner know that my plan is to take all this information back to shop, do a load calculation, select equipment, draw a quick piping schematic for the purposes of a generating a material list, analyze what they have, the ways to improve it, crunch the numbers, double check it, type up the proposal, and then pause sometimes for hours before I added the final cost. How's that for a run-on sentence! I also wanted to be certain that when it's all said and done, my company is walking away with a profit. Profit is a necessity to what we're doing. Vacations, savings accounts, education, weddings, investments, and the fact that you must render unto Caesar quarterly, somebody's got to pay for all of that so make sure you're covered.

Another thing, you've got to be yourself. If you're anything like me, you've never had a salesperson on staff. You wore that hat as well as you wore your hard hat. The way I see it; I'm a mechanic, a hydronic designer, a pipefitter, an electrician, and a controls expert all rolled into one. Who better to evaluate some old clunker of a boiler and a rat's nest of control wiring than a guy like that? A professional salesman? Not in my world.

I have nothing against salespeople. Well, that's not entirely true but most "Sales Engineers" are likely going to quote a piece of equipment and that's it. Cut loose the old one, slide in the new one, collect a check, enforce the tailgate warranty, and be on their way. And the customer is not much better off than they were at the start of the day.

They focus too much on collecting checks rather than doing a thorough, well planned, precisely executed job. In my experience if you focus on the latter, your work and your reputation will become your best sales tool, not the words spewing out of your mouth.

There's more. There's always more. Treat every customer or potential customer like you're being graded because you are from the minute you pull up to their home or place of business, you are being evaluated.

Is this guy being straight with me?

Does she know how important this is to us?

Can I trust them with this big investment?

Will they honor their warranties?

Are they skilled craftsmen?

It's not too far-fetched to think that they're considering these things. If you behave like a professional, you have nothing to worry about.

Treat every customer or potential customer as if you'll need them for a reference because some day you will.

Be yourself. I wore Red Wing boots, jeans, and a company shirt on these calls. No pretense. As my freaky forearmed, spinach chugging, cartoon buddy says, "I am what I am."

Be prepared. Flashlight. Tape measure. iPad with photos of previous jobs. References. Business card. Note pad and pen.

Health and safety issues. Point them out and assure them you'll address them properly.

Tell them how you plan to attack the job, what you plan to do, and how that is going to benefit them.

Let them know a little bit on how you operate once on the jobsite; you're going use clean tarps, nobody is going to smoke, we'll ask before playing a radio and if you say yes, we'll play it at a low volume. When we leave at the end of each day, we'll leave the place cleaner than we found it.

If they ask you a question and you don't know the answer, say you don't know the answer. Because if you throw some WAG out there, they're going to sense it; and you may lose all credibility at that point. Assure them that you'll check into it and get back to them. There's no shame in being honest or not knowing every answer to every question.

There are many of us in this great trade that are heavily invested and dedicated to their craft. And it's one of those industries where the education never stops. But at the end of the day it's a business and a business must make more money than it spends to be successful. Success in sales is essential in that endeavor.

My intent is to give you another way of approaching sales and the notion that it's ok to think outside the box. Not too many of us have a bachelor's degree in sales or marketing. That's ok. We have a master's degree in ourselves and HVAC.

C H A P T E R 11 – The Folly of Youth

1981; that's the year I began working with the tools for pay. I was 20 years old and they reimbursed me a whopping $4.50 per hour for my efforts. I did not graduate from college, but I did have almost two years at a university and another year at an HVAC trade school so $4.50 an hour wasn't anything to brag about. I had made a lot more on previous jobs.

It didn't matter though. This is what I wanted to do. Trade school convinced me of that. I got an A on everything I did in the shop and in the classroom and it came easy to me. My career course was etched in granite. I figured I learned most everything a technician could possibly need to know in the halls of Coyne American Institute. I could not have been more wrong.

I knew that with 100% certainty after my first few months of work. I saw guys fabricating complicated sheet metal fittings, bending conduit, pulling wire, installing circuit breakers, threading pipe, diagnosing bad circuit boards, scaling 40' extension ladders like they were walking up a flight of stairs, and ripping out old boilers faster than I thought possible.

It was an incredible experience, those early days, and I did my best not to screw up anything or tick off the guys who were training me. I'm not sure I accomplished either, but I started making lists to reduce that chance. I made lists of everything I didn't know how to do and other lists about things that I knew little about.

For example, I didn't like not knowing how to snap in a circuit breaker. I know now that it's a relatively simple thing to do, but when you're a 20-year old kid looking inside an electrical panel for the first time, it can be scary. Wires everywhere, buss bars just waiting for my hand to slip and fry me like an Irish kid on a hot summer beach. This was the very first thing on my list, followed by all the other tasks mentioned above.

I wasn't always successful the first time. A couple months after I started, they put me out on my own doing service calls and installing water heaters and humidifiers. My first humidifier took me 4 hours and so did my first water heater and I'm certain neither of them were a work of art.

My biggest flop was, quite literally, a flop. I had a late afternoon no heat call in Barrington, IL. I went there feeling confident that I'd have this thing up and going in no time. I knew they had a Lennox Pulse furnace and I was already well schooled on these noisy beasts. Within 5-10 minutes, I was close to a diagnosis. The pressure switch wasn't closing after the draft inducer blower ramped up to full speed. The snow was coming down heavy and I was willing to bet my $140 paycheck that the intake pipe on the roof was plugged.

Another chance to whittle away at the checklist! This would be my first solo attempt at setting up an extension ladder against this two-story brick house. Jacket, gloves, boots, hat, and hood on, ready to brave this frigid Chicago afternoon. Setting the ladder was a breeze. Carrying my steel toolbox up to the top of the ladder? Not a problem for this seasoned 3-month veteran. Stepping from the ladder to the roof? As big a problem as you could possibly imagine. Not even in my worst nightmare, could I envision what was about to happen next.

As my right foot was in mid-air approaching the 7/12 pitched snow-covered roof, the ladder slid out from under me crashing onto the icy driveway. I dropped my toolbox and then gravity, in all its infinite power, dropped me. The ladder, the toolbox, and then me. That's the order in which we hit the driveway two stories below. Luckily for me, I didn't land on either. Unluckily for me, I landed on a concrete driveway. But it could have been worse. It can always be worse. There was 5-6" of snow on the ground and I was bundled up like my wife when our house is 68 degrees. I stuck my landing perfectly. If there were judges present, I'm sure they all would have been holding signs with 10s on them. I landed 100% horizontally on my back; and my hood, hat, and the snow level shielded my skull from splattering. I had the wind knocked out of me for what seemed like days, but that was it. Other than my banged-up ego, I survived the crash entirely. There wasn't a single scratch or bruise on my entire body.

The intake pipe was indeed plugged, and it stayed that way for the night. I just disconnected it inside to get them heat, and me and another guy returned the next day to the scene of the crime without yellow tape. It would have been nice to know that was an option earlier.

I made a series of mistakes on this one.

I should have never attempted to scale a pitched roof with that much snow on it in the first place. It's one of the most foolish things I've done in my life. There is no defense of my ill-advised decision that day, but I felt a lot pressure to succeed and my boss was insanely difficult to please. No self-imposed pressure or pressure from anyone else should lead you into doing something unsafe or stupid.

Secondly, whenever you use an extension ladder you absolutely must secure it at the top. All kinds of really bad things can go wrong if you don't.

Finally, if you must use an extension ladder make sure the bottom is also secure. If there's grass there, use it and dig the ladder's foot claws into the turf. If it's a commercial building and the concrete is slippery for whatever reason and you have nobody there to hold the ladder, go to plan B. Plan B for me was to wedge the bottom of the ladder against the bottom side or rear of my truck. I didn't check with OSHA on this one, but it did keep me alive all these years.

I was 20 with 90 days experience. Honestly, some of those that trained me weren't the greatest. Nowadays, safety is an integral part of every trade curriculum and we all should be grateful for that. At the end of the day, we all must take responsibility for our actions, so I'll own what I did that day. I just wished I would have had safety and "don't be a knucklehead" on my list.

C H A P T E R 12 – We Don't Have One

I hated hearing that. But that's the answer I was hearing far too often. It went something like this.

"Hey Ralph, run out to the truck and grab a 3/4" black iron, street 90."

10 minutes later, Ralph comes back and says, "Yeah boss, we don't have one. I checked everywhere."

"Are you sure?"

"100% positive. It's nowhere to be found."

This is the kind of thing that can't happen repeatedly, if you want to be profitable, efficient, and running on schedule. Nothing changes if nothing changes.

I can honestly say that I was never blessed with any extraordinary talent or skill. Like most, I've had to grind it out and scrape for everything I have. Sure, I would love to be able to shred a guitar like Eddie Van Halen or dominate baseball the way Mike Trout does, but it was clear early on that I was never destined to be on the cover of Rolling Stone or Sports Illustrated.

No big deal, not too many of us are so we carve out our niche as best we can.

The way I etched my path was through a work ethic that was handed down to me by my parents, an eye for detail, and ways of organizing things that the DSM, The Diagnostic Manual of Statistics and Mental Disorders, would surely define as simply strange.

True, it's possible that I organize things a little more than most, but it's made me very efficient in both my personal and professional life. And I've found an interesting byproduct in the actual practice of being organized. While sorting 1\2" copper sweat fittings, I find myself solving other problems while doing so. Let's face it, it doesn't take much thought in distinguishing an elbow from a coupling, so your mind can be working on other things at the same time.

I hear a lot of people in the trades say they don't have the time to organize their truck or their shop. I say they don't have the time not to. Most of us don't figure this out until our hair is grey or we're consuming Advil like we owned stock in it. Others never figure it out. I want to help you get there sooner than I did. When I was younger, I wasted a lot more steps than I needed to. Back and forth to the truck, back and forth to the supply house. It was chaotic. Efficiency and chaos don't work well together.

For the last 15 years or so, I never felt rushed or felt any kind of anxiety to get the job done right now. Trust me, I was productive, and I expected my guys to be productive, but running around like a madman no longer made any sense to me. Organizational skills will save you time, aggravation, and money. I've seen guys going out to their trucks and emptying three 5-gallon buckets to find one single fitting. Multiply that by only a few times and you're already having a bad day.

Maybe as we grow older, we do it out of necessity because every wasted step or minute costs us more than what it did when we were younger. The back, knees, hips, lungs, and most every other body part takes a beating in the trades. Ask me how I know that? I've had a desk job for over a year now and I'm still dealing with major back problems. But I can tell you this with absolute certainty, the earlier you start working intelligently, the better off you're going to be at 60.

I applied my organizational skills across every aspect of being an installer, serviceman, and mechanical contractor. Shop, truck, desk, computer files, and record keeping. The shop and truck stuff are infinitely more fun for me to talk about so that's where I'm heading. And most of us are using the tools, pipe, fittings, and parts so it just makes sense to hit that first. Right?

First off, keep an inventory of what replacements parts you're carrying. And re-stock that evening or the next morning. There's nothing worse than going on a night service call, diagnosing a cracked Lochinvar flame sensor, and finding out you don't have a Lochinvar flame sensor when your company installs hundreds of that Lochinvar boiler. Your night just got longer because now you're heading back to the shop to grab one, assuming one is at the shop. Your customer isn't going to be pleased either because now they must stay up another hour or so, and they have to go to work in the morning. I'm going to go out on a limb and say the boss isn't going to be thrilled either. I speak from personal experience that as a former serviceman, that last one is a tough conversation to be a part of. Sure, you overlooked the fact that you didn't have a common part on your truck, but you also worked most of the night so hopefully your manager or boss is able to see the big picture. Just try not to make a habit of it. Repeating the same mistakes is never good.

I was really, really focused on the fittings, hardware, and other small essentials that were needed on a service or install truck. At first, I used Stanley storage boxes until Milwaukee came out with their infinitely better stackable boxes. I usually kept 20 to 30 of those on my truck. That's a lot, I know. But having a guy run for a Tapcon screw, 1" ProPress fitting, 3/4" sweat ball valve, or a tube talon in the middle of the day, in the middle of a job is the very definition of wasting time and money. Don't waste time and money. It's bad business. Spend a little more money on the inventory, and the means to keep that inventory organized, on the front end so you're not spending three times that amount on the back end. Another thing I did was label the Milwaukee boxes for obvious reasons. The less time looking for something, the more time spent knocking out the job. Trust me, there's so much less stress knowing you have what you need and knowing where to find it.

For pipe, strut, and rod. I did what most everyone else has been doing forever. I had a couple of 6" PVC tubes on the ladder with lockable covers. For the most part, I stocked 1/2", 3/4", 1', and 1 1/4" copper pipe, 3/4" PVC, 1/2" conduit, 7/8" strut, 1 5/8" strut, and 3/8" threaded rod. This would get us through most jobs, but it wasn't unusual to need copper up to 2" as well. You do you. Stock what you'll commonly use.

Another thing that I kept on my truck was a box of meticulously organized 3 ring binders. The box sat between the two seats in my van and had a top that I could use to keep my lunch and other things on. I kept a binder for most every mod-con boiler that we commonly serviced or installed. Yes, we all use smart phones and tablets but when I needed answers right now and was getting poor connectivity, I wanted a backup plan. The less time spent being aggravated was more time spent on solving the problem at hand. For me, the usual binders were Viessmann, Lochinvar, Weil McLain, Peerless, Burnham, Buderus, Mitsubishi Mini-Splits, and

Trane TAM9 air handlers. If you've ever worked on a TAM9, you'll understand. If you intuitively understand the TAM9, you're not an HVAC Technician. You're an HVAC Savant. If you assumed that I labeled the binders too, you would be correct.

I saved the best for last because most of us love our tools.

Here's how I did it. Up front, in the cab, on top of the box of 3 ring binders, I kept a small Veto Pro Pac TP-3 service tool pouch. With just those few tools, I could diagnose most problems within a boiler room. Repair a bunch of them too. I did it this way because I didn't know what I was going to run into, and I didn't want to be hauling in half the truck for no reason.

If the repair were more involved, I'd bring in the Big Guns. 2 large Veto Pro Pac bags which had almost every service tool I could possibly need. One of the was focused on control and component repair and replacement while the other was focused strictly on pipe repair. The one for the pipe repair had tape, dope, flux, solder, glue, primer, sand cloth, fitting brushes, and on and on and on. Fewer trips to the truck meant the more energy I had throughout the day, the more efficient I was, the less hurried I was, the happier the customer was, and the next customer waiting for me.

You see how this works? There's no downside to being on top of your game and to do that you need to be organized. One more thing and then I'll shut up. Get a cart. Please. One with a top shelf and a bottom shelf about three feet long. Oh, if only I would have done this earlier. I didn't start until my last 3-4 years in the field. This is, hands down, the one single thing that will save your back and knees more than any other tool you own. Time too. Except, of course, your power tools.

C H A P T E R 13 – Radiant Floor Design

There's no way I can cover a complete radiant design in this column or this entire magazine for that matter. There's a lot to know. Most design manuals are in the 200-300 pages range. But I'll do my best to hit the highlights and the things to avoid at all cost.

I was part of a basement radiant installation as an apprentice in 1982. It was the first time I dipped my toes in on a hydronic radiant floor. My job was simple. I had to tie strap the tubing as fast as humanly possible to the 6" x 6" wire mesh and get the others lunch when they were hungry. It wasn't long after that, that I realized my boss and his lead installer did everything as wrong as wrong can be.

How did I know this?

Because over the course of the next two winters, I spent enough time at that house for it to qualify as my home address. The system never worked. Not at startup, not a week later, and certainly not a year and a half later when I moved on to a company opting for shorter loop lengths. It's there that I started digging into radiant heating books to see what went wrong on that job in.

Here's a short list of what I remember as the biggest mistakes:

- 1/2" loops of tubing, 1000' feet long.
- Polybutylene tubing used without a heat exchanger, or non-ferrous pipe and components.
- Couplings being used randomly on kinked tubing that was to be imbedded in 4 inches of concrete.
- A cast iron boiler was used without protection against low return water temperatures, such as 4-way mixing valve.
- The tubing was never pressure tested before the pour.
- No insulation was used beneath the tubing and half of the basement was of the walkout variety.

Those six things are more than enough to kill the radiant panel, the boiler, and all the other components. I'm not sure how the ensuing lawsuit went, but South Barrington is at the top of high society suburbs of Chicago, so I know the homeowners did not go gently into that good night. I still remember the homeowner's name and I can't remember what I had for dinner last night. That's how epic this train wreck was.

My goal is to help you avoid these pitfalls and lead you in the direction of a successful radiant floor design and install; each, and every time.

Like any successful hydronic design, there should be a step by step process to make sure you've covered everything you need to cover. It's a lot easier to get it right the first time rather than having to correct it after the fact. And with radiant floor heating, after the fact can be a nightmarish ordeal. Tubing is almost never easily accessible so correcting loop lengths, kinks, and leaks usually requires demolition of some sort; and nobody is going to be happy about that.

REHAU manifold.

The other outcomes of poor design could include expensive stone or tile cracking, concrete cracking, hardwood floor failures, boiler short cycling, boiler inefficiency due to high return water temperatures, early boiler failure, cold spots, lack of comfort one way or the other, and the need for oversized pumps.

Below is the way I was taught by some folks much smarter than I am, so I'm going to pass along that information because it works, and we need our systems to work. This method is quick, accurate, and shows you how to do it by hand. Radiant design software, at the end of the day, is better because of how quickly you can manipulate the numbers and the fact that you can generate professional reports and material lists from them. But I think it's worth knowing how the numbers work.

- **Perform a Room by Room Heat Loss Load Calculation** – Block loads usually don't work very well with radiant floor design because it's rare to have the same type flooring throughout. You can have two identical rooms with identical heat losses but may require different supply water temperatures because of the finished floor. Heavy padding and thick carpeting are going to require higher water temperatures than one with tile or stone. Avoid them if possible.
- **Determine Room Thermostat Setpoint Temperature** – This is usually 65°F -70°F for radiant floor systems, 65°F being the most common.
- **Determine Room Square Feet** – Length x Width = Area
- **Determine the BTU/h needed per square foot per room** – Simply divide the room heat loss by the room square footage.

- **Determine Floor Surface Temperature** – Once you know the Thermostat Setpoint Temperature and the BTU/h/sf, you can easily determine the Floor Surface Temperature by using this formula:
Floor Surface Temperature = (BTU/h/sf ÷ 2) + Setpoint Temperature
Example- Setpoint = 65°
   Necessary BTU/h/sf = 20
   Constant for radiant floors = 2
   65 + 20/2 = 65 + 10 = 75 Floor Surface Temperature
- **Choose Installation Method** – Extruded aluminum plates, staple up or suspended tube (bad ideas), 4" concrete pour, 1.5" concrete overpour, and knobbed mats are just a few examples.
- **Choose Tube Type and Size –** As far as tube type is concerned, I like to stick with PEX A because if you accidentally kink the tubing, it can be restored to its original shape by gently heating it. Heat guns are fine. Torches are not. I'm also a big fan of Pex-Al-Pex. Once you form the bend, it stays bent without fear of it coming back and whacking you in the face.
The installation method will determine the tubing size. Concrete is typically 1/2" and extruded plates can be 3/8" or 1/2" depending on your preference. 3/8" is much easier to work with, but the maximum loop lengths are shorter due to greater pressure loss.
- **Determine Floor Covering R Value** – Charts for these values are available at tubing manufacturer's websites such as REHAU, Uponor, or Mr. Pex.
- **Determine Design Delta T** – This is the target temperature difference between the supply water temperature and the return water temperature, typically 10°F in residential applications.
- **Determine Tube Spacing** – Most residential applications are going to be 6", 8", 9", or 12" depending on the type of room, the room's BTU/h needs, and the installation method. Here's how I normally attack this – For basements it's almost always 12" on center, extruded plates is always 8", and concrete overpours vary between 6", 9", and 12" depending on the room heat loss and how low I want the supply water temperatures to be.
- **Determine Supply Water Temperature** – Four factors will provide us with this number –
1. BTU/h/sf *2.* Design Delta T *3.* Installation Method *4.* Tube spacing. Charts are provided by tubing manufacturers.
- **Determine Active Loop Lengths and Leader Lengths** – Loop lengths are calculated by using these multipliers:
   o 12" on center tubing x 1.0
   o 9" on center tubing x 1.33
   o 8" on center tubing x 1.5
   o 6" on center tubing x 2.0
   Leader or Tail Lengths is the just distance between the room and the manifold x 2.
   You'll find some small differences in the recommended loop lengths, but you'll be safe with these.
   3/8" tubing – 200'
   1/2" tubing – 300'
- **Determine Total GPM** – This one is easy too.
GPM = Heat Loss in BTU/ (Design Delta T x 500)
Example: 100,000/ (10 x 500) = 100,000/5000 = 20 GPM
500 is constant that comes from these values and equation:
There are 8.33 pounds in one gallon of water.
There are 60 minutes in an hour.
And 1 is the specific heat of water.

8.33 x 60 x 1 = 499.8

499.8 rounds out to 500

- **<u>Determine GPM per Loop</u>** – Total GPM / Number of Loops = GPM per Loop
- **<u>Determine Pressure Loss or Head Loss</u>** – This is where most guys might get overwhelmed a bit, but don't. It's not necessary. There are so many calculators and tools to use that make it easy on you, but my favorite is the RadPad. The RadPad was originally made available by the RPA, The Radiant Panel Association, now known as the Radiant Professional's Allegiance. This tool does it all and if I can figure it out, so can you. On the back side of this slide calculator you just set the *Flow per Tube* in *the Nominal Tube Size* window and then read the *Pressure Loss* above the *Tube Circuit Length.*

  A quick example and I mean quick because it took me less than 10 seconds to get answer.

  If my 1/2" tubing has a GPM of .6 and my tube circuit length is 265 feet, my pressure loss is roughly 4.3'. It's that easy.

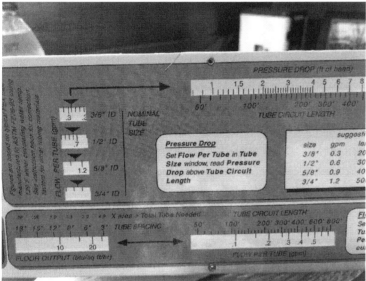

Invaluable tool.

Get the app here - https://www.drakeip.com/RadPad/index.html

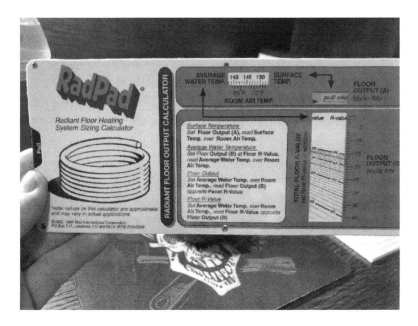

Let's run through a complete design. This is exactly what I described above shown in a single snapshot summary. It shows what you need, the way you arrive at that need, and how you arrive at the result.

	Radiant Design Short Form		
1	Room BTU/h Requirement	Load Calculation	8370
2	Room Setpoint Temperature	By Choice	65
3	Room Area	27.35' x 17' =	465
4	BTU/h per Square Foot	8370 ÷ 465 =	18
5	Floor Surface Temperature	65 + (18/2) =	74°F
6	Installation Method	By Choice	4" Concrete Pour
7	Floor Covering R-Value	By Choice	1/2" Ceramic - 0.45
8	Design Delta T	By Choice & App.	10°F
9	Tubing Size	By Choice & App.	1/2"
10	Tubing Spacing	By Choice & App.	12"
11	Tubing Length	Measured	232.5'
12	Leader Length	Measured	50
13	Number of Loops	By Choice	2
14	Total GPM	8370 ÷ (10 x 500) =	1.7
15	GPM per Loop	1.7 ÷ 2 =	0.85
16	Supply Water Temperature	Manufacturer's Chart	95°F
17	Loop Feet of Head or Pressure Loss	RadPad App	6.5' *
* When figuring feet of head, only the longest loop is considered. In this case, we have two loops of the same length, same size tubing, and same GPM so the head is in equal for each loop. The Total GPM, 1.7, is used when selecting a circulator.			

Something like this makes you dig in a little further than using software and helps you understand the process and math better. I know it did for me.

Things to Know & Avoid

- As I mentioned earlier, different floor coverings are often going to require different supply water temperatures. That said, do your best to limit the amount of different water temperatures you'll use in your design. Good mixing valves and circulators aren't cheap. If I have design supply water temperatures with 10°-15°F of one another, I'll consider using a number in between if there are no foreseeable problems.
- Educate your customer and understand their expectations.
    - A well-designed system may not produce floors that will always warm their toes. Be sure they know that.
    - If they intend to put area rugs on the radiant heated floors, they need to know they're blocking their only heat emitter. The bigger and thicker the rug, the worse it will be.
- Do your homework on hardwood floors. Check with the Radiant Professionals Allegiance and the National Wood Flooring Association.
- If the floor covering is tile or stone, I'd recommend an anti-crack membrane be installed by the flooring contractor.
- Insulate below your radiant floor panel, no matter what type you choose. Buyer beware, not all insulation performs as advertised. Follow generally accepted industry standards.
- If your loop lengths are not within 10% of each other, be sure to use manifolds that allow for balancing.
- Always pressurize your tubing and manifolds to 60 PSI as soon as they're installed.
- Keep in mind that if you use a glycol/water mixture, you'll need more pump. The Specific Heat of water is 1.0. The water/glycol mixture is at least 10% higher.

- When installing tubing on top of the subfloor for a 1.5" overpour, be careful of not running all of your homeruns in the common hallway. If you do so, the hallway will overheat and that's probably where your thermostat is located. I like to drill and run them under the floor. If that's not possible, insulate the majority, if not all the tubing. Your room by room load calculation will dictate how much to insulate.

- The closer you keep your on-center tube spacing, the lower supply water temperatures you'll need.

- Maximize your modulating condensing boiler efficiency by getting your return water temperatures as low as possible. The lower the RWT, the more the boiler will be in condensing mode. The longer the boiler is in condensing mode, the more efficient it will be.

- There's no need to install tubing beneath kitchen cabinets or appliances, but keep your eyes peeled for the last-minute desk niche that's added to the cabinetry. You'll want tubing there. Ask me how I know that. It was an oversight of mine in 1995 and I was constantly reminded of my 2' x 2' mistake.

You don't want to be on the wrong end of litigation so if you choose to become a radiant contractor, go all in. Read, go to seminars, ask questions, listen, and learn and you'll never have that to worry about it.

CHAPTER 14 – Are you the Curious Sort?

I am and always have been, especially when it comes to HVAC parts and equipment. It was the mid 90's when I decided that hydronics was going to be my specialty so I devoured every book and every video I could on the subject. There was a lot to be learned and taking things apart and putting them back together taught me as much as anything.

If I replaced a part that had failed and I wanted further proof of just what went wrong, I'd perform a "part autopsy" on it. I wanted to know how it failed and why it failed. You had to pick your spots for these mad scientist procedures because there's only so much time in a week, but for me it was fun and educational. I've never denied being a heating geek.

Just a few years ago, we had two newly installed Caleffi zone valves that appeared to have failed in a partially open position. The two associated zones were overheating whether there was a call for heat or not. I told my tech to replace the actuators and see if that solves the problem. It did, but it wasn't sitting right with me. We never had a problem with these valves before and now we have two on the same job right next to each other? There was something else going on and I wasn't about to let it go. I needed to know what that something was.

Back at the shop a few days later, under the glow of bench lights and a stationary 4x magnifying glass, I popped open the actuator covers and started taking a close look at everything. There it was in plain magnified sight, two of the smallest solder balls you'll ever see jamming up the valve mechanism. It wasn't much, but just enough to keep them in a partially open position. I would've never guessed it. We had preassembled the near boiler piping board in the shop, so it must've happened while piping on the job? This little bit of research avoided an embarrassing warranty denial since it was clearly our fault. In my early years, the supply house counter guys used to tell me about all the parts they would get back with nothing wrong with them. Or worse yet, it was the tech's fault. I guess that stuck with me. Who wants to be that guy? Not me.

Early in my career on Sunday mornings before anyone else in the house was up, I'd head over to where my company kept old equipment, waiting to be picked up by the scrappers. I had a lot to learn at that point so any LWCO, three-piece circulator, aquastat, Penn pilot safety valve, or boiler gauge I could get my paws on was going to help in me in that endeavor. I was 21 at the time, newly married, and we lived in a single bedroom apartment with one walk-in closet. On my wife's side of the closet, there was a gallery of shoes on the floor. My side? One pair of work boots, a pair of gym shoes, and a complete inventory of antiquated boiler parts saved from the scrap heap.

If my dirty rotten boss was going to send me out to replace a coupler and motor mounts on Bell & Gossett Series 100 pump without first showing me how to do it, I was going to practice on my own time. Some may think I was fool for doing that on my own dime. Thing is, I was investing in myself as much as I was the company I worked for at the time. Improving your game is an inside job.

When I got older and had a shop and a garage, I went as far as adding disconnect switches with test leads on my bench used exclusively for testing. I could test and check almost anything that was 24 volt, 120 volt, or 230 volt so long as it didn't exceed the ampacity of the circuit and it's overload protection. You learn a lot of interesting things doing that. Plus, let's face it, it's cool. Clipping a couple of alligator clips on a motor, gas valve, zone valve or hot surface ignitor and seeing and hearing them live or die is entertainment for me. It's even more entertaining when you see a valve start to open, then slow up, make some noise, and then finally continue on, or just flat out die, just to find a loose wire or a poorly soldered connection.

Bench test setup.

Tearing down circulators can be the most telling. Worn impellers, damaged bearings, and just the overall abuse we put these things through. Water quality is more important now than ever before with the advent of modulating condensing boilers. For further information on this, please read the 18th edition of Caleffi *idronics* found on Caleffi's website. The worst cases I've seen are on glycol systems where the water/glycol mixture has never been maintained properly, or ever for that matter. Nothing screeches and screams trouble like this.

Pump corrosion.

This was a functioning pump, but I'd never call it fully functioning. I'm not even sure why I unbolted. It was a typical maintenance call. Maybe it was just curiosity? I'm glad I did though. Once the owner saw it, he was all in on replacing it, cleaning the system, adding a conditioner, and refilling with a fresh 40% glycol/water mixture.

Here's another example why it's important to be inquisitive. We just finished a simple cast iron boiler replacement in a brick bungalow in Chicago. The house was in the middle of a gut rehab and a week later we get a call for no heat. The owner says it just stopped working for no reason and there was no display on the Beckett control.

I send a guy down there with a new control in hand just in case. Sure enough, the control was toast. But why? Turns out the demo crew just started tearing out plaster and wire mesh and everything else that got in their way without bothering to turn the power off. Well, they pulled the thermostat wire out with the wall and shorted it to the mesh and armored cable inside the wall. New thermostat wire was pulled, new thermostat, and a new control. All's good, right?

Not so much. Owner says that it should be covered under warranty because the boiler is only a week old.

Well, I like to think that I'm a reasonable guy and a reasonable guy doesn't leave money on the table when there's hundreds of dollars, worth of time and labor, on that table. Take pictures and don't be afraid to pop open a part to prove your point. We took pictures of the Beckett control, the digital thermostat, and the exact spot where the wire got cooked by his reckless, wrecking crew. Once I showed him all the pictures, he cut me a check on the spot.

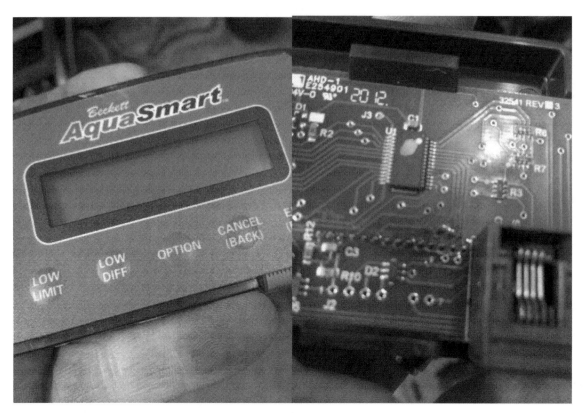

Clearly a fired circuit board.

Is there a limit to my curiosity? Not really, other than the limitations of time that we all face. My three daughters are long into their careers with kids of their own and I'm inching closer to retirement, so I have plenty of time to knock around in my shop at home.

A couple years ago we replaced an air handler on a Unico high velocity air conditioning system and the Trane outdoor condensing unit. The system was installed in the fall of 1989 and still operating fairly well despite being inefficient; 8 SEER if I'm not mistaken. I've heard these bad boys are hard to stop and I've always been a sucker for cutaways, so my next step was as clear as this old system's sight glass.

This 1989 Trane compressor never stopped.

Did I learn much here? Not really, but that's the way it goes sometimes. The inside of this tin can smelt clean and the windings looked like they had years left in them. Next time I get my hands on a Trane Climatuff compressor, I'm going to cut lower on the can to where the real mechanical stuff resides. That's what curiosity is all about, digging in and seeing what makes these things we work on every day, tick. It's fun and you're likely going to learn something from it. What's not to like about that?

CHAPTER 15 – One Step Program

It started innocently enough. It was just one every now and then. Then, it became a daily routine; an obsession if you will. Once I had one, I couldn't stop myself. I had to have more. It got to the point where I'd go to any length just to get one more. I knew I had a problem but wasn't sure what to do about it. Step 1, I guess; admitting you have a problem. But I had no intention of stopping. It was just too much fun. Still is.

I began collecting heating paraphernalia about a week and a half after I started my first job in the industry. It started small like most habits; a boiler data plate here, a boiler name tag there. Before you knew it, I was scavenging old equipment for antiquated parts and calling friends in the business to see if they had any I could score from them. More, more, more. I had built up a tolerance so that I could have 10, 20, or even 100 and I could still handle it. Truth is, not all habits are bad. This is the part where my vocation becomes my avocation as well.

One of my all time is favorites is this century old American Radiator Company coal fired water heater. On the data plate it's described as an Ideal Hot Water Boiler, Number 50, Series 1B. It was connected to a 30-gallon storage tank from two 1" tappings on the back of the heater. Not only did the owner let me have this, she tipped me $100.00 for getting it out of her basement. I felt like I won the lottery that day.

Coal fired water heater.

I have a few of the Ideal Fitter Handbooks and have been unsuccessful at finding the specs for this model.

American Radiator swag has always been something I've kept my eyes out for. Kewanee Boiler is another one I love to get my hands on. Chicago apartment buildings and churches are veritable museums for Kewanee. They're everywhere and many of them are still in service. Many of the brickset boilers have been long retired are still sitting there in the basements because the cost of removal is just too expensive for most. For heating junkies like me, it's perfect. The building owners, typically, are grateful for any piece of the old beasts you can get out of there. Kewanee, Illinois is where these beauties were manufactured; a very small town about 3 hours west of Chicago. It only makes sense that we have so many of them here, shipping costs would be minimal.

Here's a picture of the actual Kewanee Type C three pass, firetube boiler where I got most of my stash. It's still sitting in the apartment building basement on Chicago's south side. A Weil-McLain 88 steam boiler replaced it just last summer. It was still operable, but repair costs were getting prohibitive, so the owners made the wise decision of replacing it.

Kewanee Boiler.

What did I grab and what did I do with it?

Most anything that had the name Kewanee on it, or the Kewanee K. After that, it went into my little shop at home where it was kept until I had time to clean it up and restore it.

This is where the fun part comes in for me. I get out the wire wheels, wire brushes, paint, paint brushes, Dremel tool, cleaning agents, nitrile gloves, and anything else I need to make these things come alive again. It can be time consuming but there's worse habits a guy could have. Right? Once I get piece done, it goes on display in my shop. It's a reminder for me of how much I enjoyed working in boiler rooms. I really did. I was in my element there.

The finished product isn't half bad either. In fact, I dig it. That sweet gauge is mounted on a real 2 x 4 from early last century.

Kewanee Swag.

The door was the harder of the two. Lots of paint and rust to remove and the lettering is always a bit of a challenge. It isn't on display yet because I lost one of the pins for the door hinges, but when I get another one it's going to serve as the door to the dartboard in my shop. Cool, right? The boiler gauge is a more delicate challenge as I like to get the face clean without removing any of the print. I have quite a few gauges, but this is my first Kewanee.

The water column and water gauge below is another one I copped off that old boiler. I even went as far as removing 90% of the rust and debris out of its guts. It's one of my favorites and also the first time I was able to grab one.

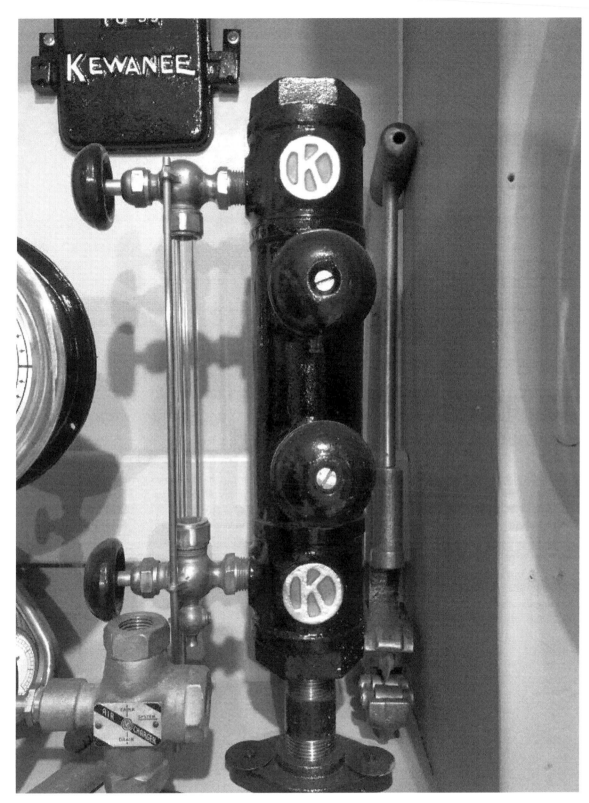

My Boiler Museum.

This next one is interesting to me because it's a fuel saving mechanism that was patented in 1920, for coal no less. I didn't know they thought about those kinds of things back then. It was a series of chains and pulleys connected to a manually adjusted flue damper to a steel plate with "buttons" as the inventor described them. By moving the chain from one button to another, you change the position of the flue damper, thereby adjusting the draft and the fire. As you can see, the buttons have screwdriver slots that can be loosened to slide them vertically for different amounts of draft.

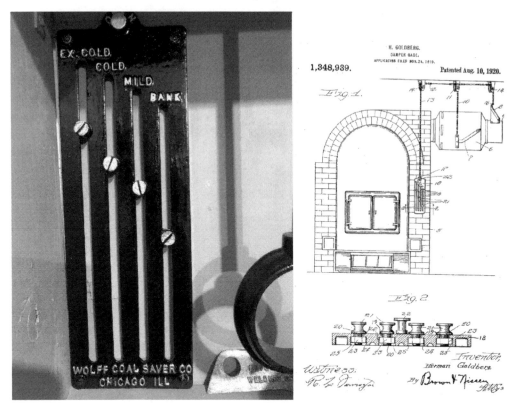

Energy efficiency in the early 1900s.

These too, are all over the city of Chicago. They've long been abandoned with just the steel wall plate and the chains dangling from the ceiling remaining. I just had to have of these. I wonder how often the owner, or the maintenance man adjusted these? Or were they just left in the open position, which is not adjustable?

The data plates and equipment name tags are much easier to get your hands on. They're on every piece of equipment you replace so why not grab them? I started on these early and glad I did. Almost all of them back in the day were made of steel, and sometimes heavy gauge steel. I have a few data plates that are 16 gauge. I usually display them on something that can be moved. A painted piece of 3/4" plywood or the like.

There were times when I got creative with the displays too, like this Craftsman toolbox where I took the time to drill holes and blind rivet them on. I must've been bored that Saturday. The Williamson Five in One and the other Williams furnace tags on there are what I cut my teeth on. Same with the Mueller Climatrol furnaces. Belt driven motors, standing pilots, and gas trains that included a separate gas regulator, main valve, and pilot valves. I wonder how many techs today could describe a Lowboy furnace?

Dual purpose tool box.

Here's the board of plates and tags that hangs in my shop. It's hung like you'd hang a picture so I can easily move it if I choose. I'm not entirely sure why there's refrigeration controls up there other than to take up space until I get some more tags.

Hydronic souvenirs.

I think there's only one plastic name tag in the bunch. The rest are stored away in a box somewhere. I'm too old school to put them on display. Maybe when they're replaced with computer generated images I'll relent and put them up somewhere.

I also collect ancient heating books with some that date back to the late 1800's, really old installation and service manuals, and antique tools that have been used in our trade. But my favorite collectible weighs about 500 pounds and has a born-on date of approximately 1865. I pulled this wrought iron tube radiator of an old church where we did a steam to hot water conversion a few years ago.

I flushed all the rust out, stripped all the paint and rust off, primed it, painted it and now its sits in our living room even though we don't have steam heat. It wasn't even that difficult to sell the idea to my wife. She likes old things. She's still with me, so there's that.

My favorite radiator.

I think you'd agree that I have this thing under control. No unmanageability. No powerlessness. No worries.

I got this.

CHAPTER 16 – The Transition

He's played in 1,114 games over the course of a 15 year career with the Chicago Blackhawks, averaging 21:56 minutes per game. He was an integral part of the three Stanley Cup winning teams and has always been a leader, both on and off the ice. He's been a player's player and a coach's dream. His #7 jersey may never hang in the Hockey Hall of Fame, but it's the only one I've bought in the last twenty years. I think that much of him. He just had shoulder surgery and is due to have both hips operated on this upcoming off-season. He's been a healthy scratch five games this year, coach's decision. Not a good sign.

Brent Seabrook is now facing what all us who work in a physically demanding job face at some point or another, the fact that his body can't take anymore punishment. Not one more hit. Not one more blocked shot. Life comes at you fast, so you best be prepared for it.

When I was a kid, I'd run through a brick wall if that's what my boss wanted me to do.

If he needed me to work 72 hours a week, I did, because if you multiply $4.50/hour by 1.5, that equals $6.75/hour, and who in their right mind is going to walk away from that kind of rare coin?

Need me to cut and thread hundreds of feet of 2" black iron pipe by hand, hang it all from a 16' ceiling by myself? Consider it done.

Work a 14-hour day, spend the next 11 hours working all night because it's winter in Chicago and people need heat, and then wrap it all up by working all day, the following day? I'm your Huckleberry.

I lived that kind of insanity for the first five years of my career, working for others. And when I decided to go out on my own, things got really nuts.

I was no longer on On-Call one week per month. I was On-Call 24/7/365. Every day, every night, of every week and month, of every year for years and years. I had three very young daughters at the time, and I was missing more important events than any caring, loving dad should. And I was both. I wouldn't even blink about working holidays. It was just another day to me.

I lived to work, and it took its toll. Don't get me wrong. It's the way I'm wired, and I enjoyed the madness in a demented sort of way. There's a lot to be said for work ethic and taking pride in a job well done. But when you've spent the better part of your life swinging steel pipe wrenches, moving cast iron boiler sections up and down stairs, working in 125 degree attics and sloppy crawlspaces; and using your back, hips, shoulders, arms, wrists, legs, and knees in ways they're not meant to be used long term, body parts are going to rebel in a painful way that causes you to take notice.

I've had two neck surgeries, one back surgery, one hip surgery, 3 hand surgeries, a knee surgery, too many concussions to count, and a shoulder surgery. Arthritis reigns supreme and breathing can be a chore now. I had no choice but to put the tools down for good if I wanted any chance of seeing my granddaughters get married someday. And I do.

I've since made the transition from boiler rooms to a desk and keyboard, and it's been the biggest challenge of my career. I loved everything about being a boiler guy. I loved the Red Wing or Timberland boots I wore, the Lee Dungaree jeans that had a pocket for everything, taking a lunch to work, creating something from nothing every day, fixing things that most couldn't, having the best tool collection around, my work truck, and everything else except the trouble of getting my body to move the last couple years. It just didn't want any part of it anymore, and I don't blame it.

So here I am today writing for PHC News and loving every minute of it. But that's not all. I needed to stay in the game even more to be happy.

So, I hung up another shingle two months ago, Minnich Hydronic Consulting & Design LLC. It just made so much sense to me, and I just couldn't deny the urge. I've been doing HVAC design work since 1987 when I did my very first Manual J Heat Loss/Heat Gain Load Calculation. I was 26 or 27 at the time and I always figured if somebody else could do something, I might be able to do it too. So, why not try. I did and I loved it. I also did my first duct design on that job with the help of someone with more experience than I had. And then in the mid 90's, I started designing all of my hydronic jobs with a little help from my industry friends until they were needed less and less.

Old School Load Calculations.

That's my goal here. I want to help you. I want to help you plan and design your projects before any wrench gets lifted or any torch is sparked up. There's nothing worse than sweating, pressing or wrenching pipes and fittings, setting boilers, wiring controls and sensors, and then finding out that it's not working the way it's supposed to work. And you want to get paid, right? Well, your customer has a death grip on their checkbook and they're not going to open it until everything is jake. Let me help you avoid that mess.

Or, maybe your time would be better spent addressing other needs of your business than designing systems?

I have 40 years of dedicated experience in the HVAC Industry as an Educator, Inspector, Technical Support Lead, Industry Columnist, and Award-Winning Contractor. Here's a sample of some of things I can do for you:

Hot Water Boiler Systems Evaluation and Design

- **Blueprint Review**
- **Evaluate condition of boiler**
- **Near boiler piping evaluation – pump location, expansion tank location, control strategy, air management and control, piping strategy, pipe sizes**
- **Evaluate heat emitters – radiators, baseboard, fan coils, radiant panels**
- **Perform Manual J heat loss load calculation based on information we gather on the building**
- **Select new boiler based on Manual J load calculation and energy efficiency**
- **Size system circulator(s) and boiler circulator(s) based on flow and head loss requirements**
- **Determine near boiler pipe sizes based on design delta T and flow requirements**
- **Determine hydraulic separator size based on minimum flow rate requirements**
- **Determine buffer tank size based on boiler turndown ratio and BTU requirement of smallest zone**
- **Determine expansion tank size based on system water volume and BTU**
- **Generate piping strategy and schematic**
- **Generate control strategy and schematic**
- **Determine outdoor reset curve based on system information and customer preferences**
- **Generate material and equipment list if needed.**

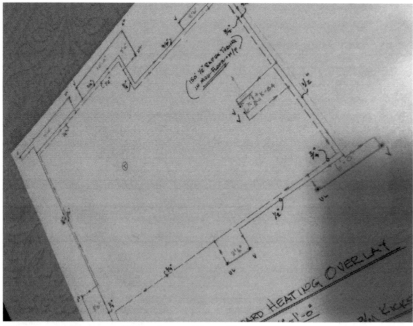

Reverse Return Burnham BaseRay

Radiant Panel System Design

- **Perform Manual J heat loss load calculation**
- **Determine BTU/square foot requirement to match heat loss**
- **Determine floor surface temperature requirements**
- **Choose projected installation method**
- **Choose tube type and size based on installation method**
- **Determine finished floor R-value**
- **Determine tube spacing based on heat loss and application**
- **Determine necessary supply water temperatures**
- **Determine loop lengths with headers**
- **Determine total GPM**
- **Determine head losses**
- **Generate material and equipment list**
- **Proposal preparation**

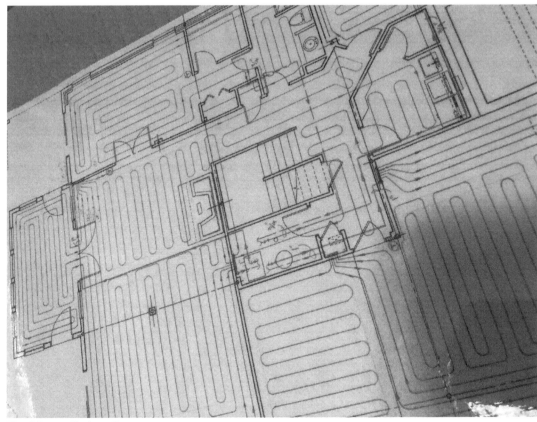

Hand Drawn Radiant Layout

The two drawings are done by hand obviously, but I also use several different computer- generated load calculations and various drawing software as well.

Combustion Analysis Training and Review
Technical Support Services
Piping Schematics
Wiring Schematics
Servicing Mod Con Boilers
Quality Control

All these things are necessary to ensure your customers are comfortable, safe, and thrilled with their new systems.

My fees are fair and reasonable. My accountant helped me put the numbers together to make sure the business is making a bit more than it spends. My overhead is low so that helps too. I charge by the hour with a minimum of 30 minutes, but I'm open to flat rate pricing for larger projects to help you with budget planning. With a monthly retainer of your choice, we can do away with the 30-minute minimum. I want to make this as painless as possible for you.

I'm not sure what's in Brent Seabrook's future, but I'm betting he's going to find a way to stay in the game too. Maybe coaching and helping others?

C H A P T E R 17 – Technology: Friend or Foe?

I must admit that I have a love hate relationship with technology.

I love that I can listen to Pearl Jam, Miles Davis, or Bruce Springsteen whenever I want because I carry around a catalog of roughly 10,000 songs on my phone. I really like the fact that I can watch Goodfellas, Shawshank Redemption, or any game of the 2016 World Series on a train ride to Chicago or a flight to Las Vegas because those and many other videos are on my iPad. I'm not complaining that I'm writing this on a keyboard rather than the typewriters I had to use in college. If I make an error while typing on my PC, which I do regularly, the computer promptly points them out to me with a variety of different colored underlines. I can go on forever about the things I love about our progress in technology because the list is endless. Oh yeah, Google maps. How can you not love that?

The other side of the coin? There's always an opposing point of view so let me recognize some of that.

I'm not crazy about the incredible amount of disinformation that's on the internet, and the willingness of people to buy what's being sold to them without doing their research regarding that information. It scares me that we have military weapons that are so sophisticated and advanced that our planet may not survive another world war. Our rights to privacy are compromised now, more than ever, and most of us go along with that because it's the price we pay for all the other things we get out of it. The upside to that is that it makes it hard for even the brilliant criminals to go off the grid.

Almost three hundred words into this and you've got to be wondering what the heck does this have to do with the heating industry?

Everything. I'm pushing 60 years old and when I started, every tool I used had this long black cord attached to it that I was required to plug into a 120-volt receptacle. Same for the lights and everything else I used back then. Plugging in, and using, a Milwaukee Hole Shooter or Sawzall wasn't that much trouble really; that is until you started tripping over all the cords in the mechanical room or if you were working in a crawlspace or attic without an outlet. Or worse yet, you're working on a new construction project and every contractor is fighting for the same, singular outlet. Nowadays, our shop vacs, drills, saws, lights, and almost every other thing I can think of right now is operated by batteries. Pipe threaders, tubing cutters, hacksaws, small air compressors, bandsaws, circular saws and so many others are available to us in a battery-operated version.

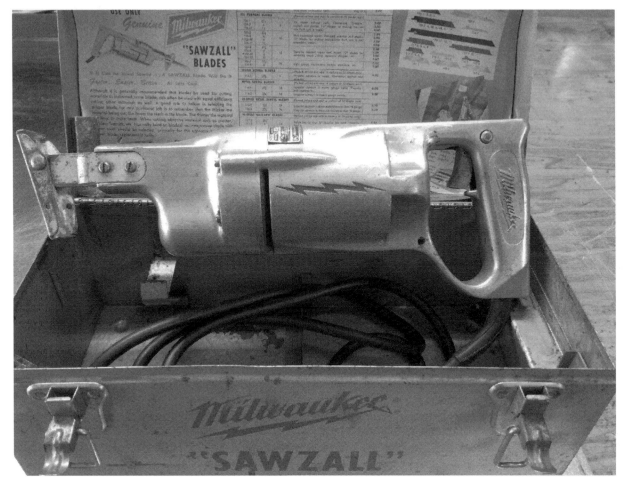

"Sawzall"

The first time I used a cordless drill was in 1985. It was a beautiful, blue Makita 7.2-volt drill and I felt like I won the tool jackpot. I'd pop a 5/16th hex head bit in it and I'd be tearing through the handfuls of RTU screws in no time. Same for working with sheet metal, except I'd be using a 1/4" hex head bit instead of the 5/16" bit. It lacked power and the batteries drained quickly, but it was a game changing move in the right direction.

9.6 volts of DC power!!!

Today, I'm putting copper pipe and copper fittings together without the aid of my torch, solder, or flux. It's so much easier and quicker than soldering and I've come to love the sound my Ridgid RP340 makes while pressing a joint. It's a reassuring noise that lets me know that there won't be any leaks, except the occasional joint I forgot to press. But that's no big deal either. You don't have to drain the system or stop the water to make the connection. Just press and move on. It's one my favorite tools and I won't let it go until the day I'm counted among the dearly departed.

An industry game changer.

My next favorite cordless tool? My Milwaukee portable, battery-operated band saws gets the runner-up prize. I use them to cut everything. Conduit, threaded rod, strut, and PVC while assembling something new; and iron pipe, electrical whips, copper, and anything else that needs to get out of my way when tearing apart a boiler room.

Really, all the cordless tools are time savers and they make all our lives easier. We get things done quicker and with the likes of press tools, we see a similar end-product regardless of who's doing the work. Sure, the arrangement of the pipe is going to be different from tech to tech, but the appearance of the joint itself will be consistent. Is that always good? I'm not sure it is. Soldering and brazing skills are examples of ways you can differentiate yourself from others. I know a lot of us older guys took a lot of pride in our ability to have clean, leak-free soldered and brazed joints. It will be a dying and lost art before long. Do you see my dilemma? I love my press tools, but now all that practice and dedication to improve my skillset seems lost. Yes, I am saying that using press tools takes some of the skill out of our trade. I can't say that's a bad thing though because of the upside of pressing. There's a lot of gray area in this world.

That's my two cents on tools.

Let's talk about boilers now, another topic of technology that causes my brain to engage in enough mental gymnastics that it makes my point of view completely unclear.

I love modulating condensing boilers. That part is crystal clear. The latter part of my career was laser focused on offering these first when they made sense for the application. I believe in reducing our carbon footprint and this is one way we can further that cause. Turndown ratios, negative pressure gas valves, stainless steel heat exchangers, sophisticated controls (some better than others), and higher efficiencies when used properly. There's a lot of fun stuff you can do with them and they'll make you more versatile and needed. And they're light! Very light. Nobody is going to wreck their back wrestling with these featherweights.

They're not for everyone though. If you're not going to commit to installing them according to the manufacturer's recommendations, commissioning them properly, and provide annual maintenance; you're doing a disservice to yourself, your customer, and the industry. They require more work and more maintenance and if you're not all in that, there will be problems. Take that bit of information to the bank. They will have service problems and likely fail prematurely. That's how bad reputations for equipment begins. We've seen it before, and that history repeats itself if you don't clearly understand the needs of new technology.

There's no shame in sticking with cast iron boilers if that's more in your comfort zone. They're relatively simple and are more forgiving when maintenance is lacking. They are reliable and will easily give you twenty five to thirty years of service, if not more. You are also at a much higher risk of back problems. Ask any old-timer. I'm two months removed from back surgery and I have two neck surgeries on my resume as well. If you can carry a couple bags of groceries, you're going to do fine carrying a modulating condensing boiler.

In 1982, I was threading two-inch pipe with a stock, 2" die, cutting oil, and pipe vise. I was installing strictly cast iron boilers and connecting the flue pipe with my Milwaukee corded drill and zip screws. My jobsite music came from an old clock radio with bad reception. Remember them? I didn't have to program a boiler control and I was less concerned about boiler water quality. It made me strong, tough; but here I am at 60, physically broken, wishing I could still be working in the boiler rooms.

If we had the technology then, that we have now, I wonder if I still would be?

CHAPTER 18 – Just Do It

I don't have too many regrets, but I wish started with steam heat earlier than I did. I had read Dan Holohan's steam books. I paid attention to the steam pro's critique of steam boiler installations posted on sites like heatinghelp.com and Instagram. I took mental and physical notes. I drew steam boiler near piping diagrams because I believe putting pen or pencil to paper enhances my ability to learn. I leaned on some steam heavyweights like Charles from some far-out rural area of Massachusetts, Frank W., Harold K., Piotr Z., and others for tips and insider information. And then, I waited. To be honest, I waited way too long. I waited because I knew the steam experts would judge my work honestly and that scared me. They are some of the most enthusiastic people in the trade and they hold the bar high. But I also knew I was missing out on something special, and my time in the field had an expiration date and it was coming fast.

Minnich Hydronic Consulting & Design
Stephen Minnich
630.291.3028
stephen.minnich@yahoo.com

STEAM PIPING

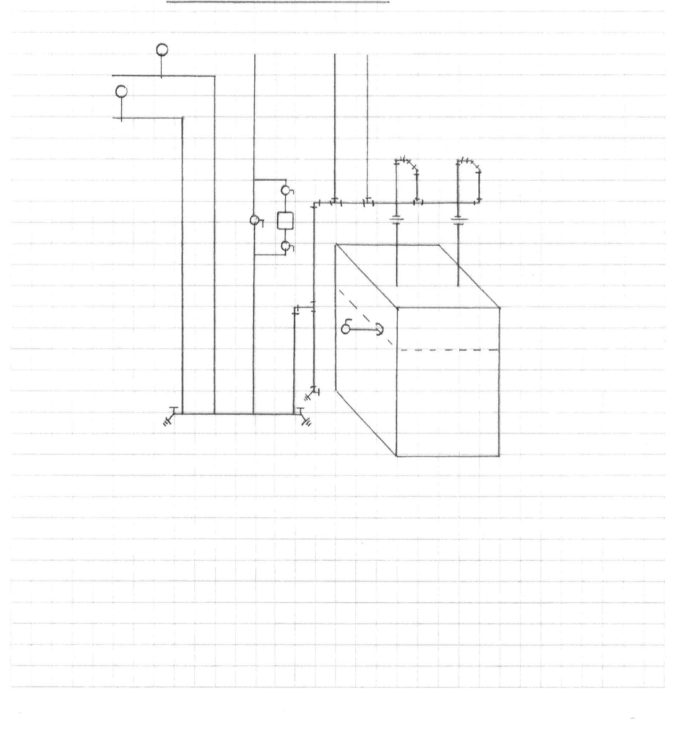

Then one day I got a request for proposal for a steam boiler replacement for an apartment building in Chicago. And I said yes, and that I'd be happy to provide you with a bid and I lost that job as fast as I ever lost a job in my life. My number, they say, was unreasonable. And looking back, I can't really argue with that. I included too much time for the learning curve that I was certain to need. I realized I needed to eat the learning curve on the first one; fair enough. My competition, friends of mine, bid this one with far less hours than I did, and it looked perfect. Their four generations of working on strictly steam heating systems will do that.

But then the day came when I bid on one and the proposal was accepted. This time it was a single-family home, so the boiler sections and pipe sizes decreased quite a bit from the commercial boiler I first bid on. It was also late summer, early fall, so there was no pressure on me to knock it out in record breaking time.

I did my due diligence and put together a material list that mimicked the manufacturer's recommended near boiler piping and then some. Once I decide to do something, I go all in. Go big or go home, I like to say. I had two full size risers coming out of this tiny Peerless boiler and then did a double drop into the header. I made certain that my main was tied into the header between the last riser and the full size equalizer. I replaced the old main vents with Big Mouth vents. After a reminder from Charles, I made sure all the returns tied in below the water line. I nailed the critical "A" dimension. The tee for my Hartford Loop started six inches below the water line and I used a close nipple out of the bull of the tee. I used ball valves and plugs for the purpose of flushing and skimming.

Drop Header Assembly

When Tim and I finished, I admit that I was proud of what we had done. We followed all the rules and it looked as good as any near boiler piping I'd ever done. Now it was time to start this beauty up. Pressuretrol set to 2 PSI and thermostat calling for heat, we switched on the boiler with homeowners eagerly watching in the boiler room along with me and Tim.

A quick side note - Whenever I wrapped up a hot water boiler installation and started it up for the first time, I would put my hand on the supply pipe. Once that got hot, I'd wait a few minutes to make sure the return pipes are warming up. Makes sense, right? Once the returns are warm, I was confident that I had adequate flow throughout the system, and we got all the air out. Force of habit I guess, not exactly science but it let me know that it was time to go upstairs and make sure all the radiators or baseboard were warming up too. A boiler guys' example of instant gratification. Once that's done, I could focus on the particulars of boiler commissioning like combustion analysis and setting the control parameters.

Back to the steam boiler - As the burner fires, I reflexively put my hand on the supply header waiting for the pipe to warm up because that's what I do. I obviously forgot about the speed at which steam travels. Those steam guys I leaned on for guidance, certainly, didn't feel the need to remind a seasoned boiler guy that steam pipes get hot infinitely faster than hot water pipes do. And not to mention the fact that they're 30-40 degrees hotter as well.

The pipe that I had a white knuckle, death grip on went from ambient temperature to skin melting hot in a New York minute. There was no gradual warm up. There was not a spare second to warn me that I was about to feel excruciating pain. It happened right now in front of everyone. The proud look on my face quickly disappeared and turned my complexion blood red with embarrassment and pain. I don't remember how I explained this misstep but aside from this humbling experience, the job went well. The heating system was quiet, the mains vented quickly, all the radiators were toasty, the burner didn't short cycle, and most importantly, the homeowners were happy.

New Boiler Piping

Why did I feel it was necessary to tell the tale of burning my hand?

The answer is because this is what this chapter is all about.

For all those years I put off getting knee deep into steam heating, for all the unnecessary fear about taking the risk of trying and learning something new, for all the money I left on the table because I had doubt about whether I could do it well enough to meet my own standards, for all that and more, I delayed doing something because I imagined all the worst things that could happen, would happen.

They didn't, not one of them.

What's holding you back from trying something new? Maybe you're that forced air guy that thinks he can't do boilers? I was a tin knocker, Tinman, my first ten years in the business and then I committed to hot water heating systems and never looked back. Maybe you're a steam guy that thinks hot water heat is getting too complicated? Well, you may be right but there's a lot of money to be made in that specialty and the boilers are much lighter, so there's that. Or, maybe your company is doing forced air, hot water heat, and steam heat, but you're not quite sure about getting into geothermal or solar? Here's the thing, there's plenty of folks that are successful in all the subcategories of our field. That means that you and I can be too if we put the work in. There'll be mistakes made. That's how we learn.

Main Vent Replacement

Sure, I felt some embarrassment and some pain in my hand. Big deal. We all get banged around a little in the trades, but don't make the mistake of borrowing trouble that's likely never going to happen. Do your homework. Invest time in training. Listen. Read. Draw piping sketches so that the image is etched in your brain. Watch the pros. Once you've done these things diligently, you're as ready as you'll ever be.

The next step is to just do it. Pick up the tools and get to work.

CHAPTER 19 – My Ideal Heating System

I've dreamt about it, planned for it, designed for it, changed it a million times, and was never quite sure it would happen. And now it is and I'm like an apprentice staring at wall full of tools in a brick and mortar supply house, drooling, and thinking of all the things I need and want.

Every house I've ever owned had forced air and I was always working so much I didn't have time to change it over. At the top of my bucket list was having my own hot water heating system, designed exactly how I wanted it, using all of my favorite products, and all the bells and whistles I could think of and there were lots of them.

It all kind of just fell together as things tend to do when you focus on doing then next right thing. Getting out of the trenches was important because it gave me more time. Along with the consulting business came requests for training from my clients, and PowerPoints bore me, so the next step was obvious. I was going to build the perfect beast. I still like to get my hands dirty and banging my knuckles never bothered me. I was focused on modulating condensing boilers, gauges, hydraulic separators, dirt mags, thermometers, ECM circs, mixing valves, radiant panels, cast iron radiators, water conditioning, low return water temperatures, long run cycles, flue gas condensation, low water cutoffs, flow balancing, bending conduit, threading gas pipe, and pressing copper.

Focused? I was more like obsessed.

There won't be much design information here. I did my due diligence and sized the boiler correctly, pipe sizing, pump selection, all that stuff. I drew the piping schematic for this project at least ten times, and not because I was making mistakes. I just kept coming up with new ideas and making changes.

Based off the somewhat final piping diagram, I put together an equipment and material list and for me, that always begins with the boiler. There are plenty of very good modulating condensing boilers on the market, but I've been partial to one for a long time, the Lochinvar Knight Fire Tube. In fact, it's the only mod con I've installed in the last eight years. Here's why I chose this one for my house and my hydronic training system.

Getting started.

Lochinvar has a strong presence in the Chicago area. That's important when selecting equipment. Lochinvar has an office/warehouse less than a mile from my home, operated by Rick Butler and Bob Butler, two great guys who have always been there for me. And working along with them is Porter Pipe and Supply. Talk about a strong presence, these guys are the heavyweight champions of PVF and Hydronics supply houses in the Chicago area. Seriously, their customer service is so forward thinking that you can walk in there any day of the week, get a free newspaper, free donuts and rolls, free tradesmen pencils, a fill rate that is always near or at 100%, AND get this – a new drive-through service. I'm not kidding you.

Presence is important, but there's more to it than that.

Back to service - If there is a problem, and there will be one on some job, somewhere, at some time; you want to make sure that your customer is taken care of. The first line of protection is the contractor. They are the ones who first get the call and they will solve the problem by themselves, most times. But parts fail and for that you rely on your supply house who, in turn, relies on the manufacturer's representative or the manufacturer themselves. There's no such thing as waiting a day or two for a part for a boiler in the middle of Chicago winter. Every time I needed something for a Lochinvar boiler, both Porter Pipe and Lochinvar met that need. And the times when things got a little bit complicated, they both went way above and beyond to uncomplicate things. That was my method of operation as a contractor so to have those companies having my back with the same mindset, made my life so much easier. For that, I am grateful.

Presence – CHECK.

Service – CHECK.

What about reliability and functionality?

As a contractor my days were long, very long. While on the job, I did my damn best to make sure everything I did was done the right way. Nobody wants to get a callback on the night of the installation, or a week or month down the road either. And you certainly didn't want to get a call for an equipment problem. We all must get up the next morning and do it all over again, so working the night before on any kind of warranty issue is bad in every way imaginable.

In these past 8 years of installing Lochinvar mod cons, I had one call the night of the installation. Truth be told, I shouldn't have gone out there that night. I repeatedly told the homeowner from Day One that his gas meter and gas line were not big enough to handle the 500,000 BTU boiler used for the new Snow and Ice Melt system. He wouldn't listen to me though. I told him I'd get dressed and head over as long he got the gas company there at the same time. We met there at 2am and sure enough the gas man told him the same exact thing I'd been telling him. I felt like I did the right thing, but I also told him this was his one and only Mulligan.

No other problems. None. Zip. Nada. That was it other than annual maintenance which I insisted on.

Reliability – CHECK.

Functionality is where Lochinvar rises above the crowd. Their control is where they shine. It's easy to navigate and it's attractive, if aesthetics means anything to you. Here are some of my favorite features:

- It allows up to three different supply water temperatures with three different outdoor reset curves.

- Ramp Delay – Six steps of time and temperature modulation that extends run time and reduces short cycling.
- Boost – Outdoor Reset feature in which the control will boost the target temperature if it hasn't been met in X amount of time. You determine what X is.
- Freeze protection features to cycle pump.
- Data logging.
- Plug and play add-on of the ConXUs control that gives you remote access to the boiler's functioning and allows you to change settings anywhere in the world.
- Allows for the use of a 0-10vDC circulator on newer models.
- Cascading of up to 8 boilers.
- Integrated DHW functionality.
- BMS Management.
- Plug and play Low Water Cut Off.
- Service and Maintenance reminders.

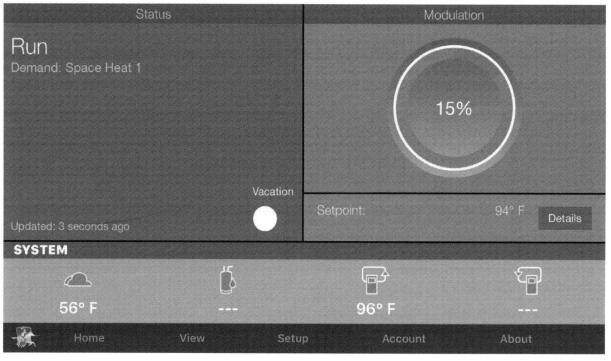

Lochinvar's ConXUs Control

One more thing about Lochinvar and then I'll move on. I've been down to their facilities in Tennessee for training, VIP Showcase, factory tour, and included in this were discussions. Discussions that involved 20 or so contractors, management, and 6-7 engineers. Management wanted to know what we thought of the Knight as contractors and if we had any suggestions on how to improve or what should be changed. That, in and of itself, is not too unusual. What is unusual is that management listened, and the engineers were taking notes. And then…they acted on our suggestions. I was genuinely and pleasantly surprised. I'd never experienced that before. They listened and acted. That was truly a game changer for me.

Alright, enough about the boiler. I want to get back to my system. Again, I could have chosen any product I wanted and could have piped it a thousand different ways. But here is what I did. It will always be a work in progress and it's my favorite toy.

The Lochinvar Knight and Porter Pipe & Supply representing.

There are some unusual things going on here, aren't there? I'll start with the obvious. Each Taco 0015 system circulator has a ½" loop piped in parallel using two ball valves on each side of a pressure gauge. I did the same for the boiler circulator. This setup allows me to see the actual head added to the fluid by the circulator, not some theoretical number. Cool, right? Not my idea, by the way. I got it from John Siegenthaler's 3rd Edition of Modern Hydronic Heating.

Here's how you do it. With the circ running, close one ball valve at a time and record the respective pressures in PSI. Now plug them into this simple formula.

H = 144(Delta P)/D

H = Head

144 = Constant

Delta P = Pressure differential between the inlet and outlet of pump.

D = Density of water at a given temperature.

Let's try it.

Inlet Pressure = 13.5 PSI

Outlet Pressure = 15 PSI

Water density @ 110 degrees F = 61.86

(144 x 1.5)/61.86 = 216/61.86 = 3.49' of head

Now you're not likely to see this in the real world other than on commercial pumps where there's pressure ports on each side of the pump. I went with one gauge to decrease the margin of error and I did it for training purposes and to satisfy the heating geek in me.

If you look closely, I not only have flow meters on the radiant manifold, but I also added Caleffi Quick Setters balancing valves with flow meters on each zone return. They make sense on almost any system and they'll act as one more visual aid for training videos.

My favorite pressure gauge is right above the expansion tank. You know the whole thing about pumping away from the point of no pressure change? Well, it's real and it's important to understand and being able to see it drives the point home. This is the only water pressure gauge on the system which remains completely unaffected when the pumps bang on. The dial just does not move. Gil Carlson was a bright guy and so was Dan Holohan for making it easier for all of us to wrap our heads around.

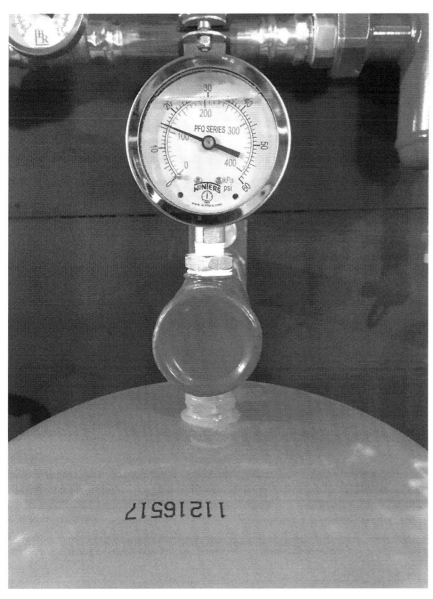

The Point of No Pressure Change

Here are few more things I did either because they were necessary or I just because I could:

- This was the first boiler installation where I went 100% ProPress. I used Viega fittings and a Ridgid RP340. My soldering skills are solid. I've had a lot of practice but if I were still in the trenches, I wouldn't go back to it. Time is big money. Fire protection is unnecessary with pressing, and I have enough scars. I'm not looking to add any more.

- I installed a ¼" gas line off the ¾" line to the boiler, complete with an Apollo ball valve and a 0-15" W.C. gauge. I'm using it for training purposes only and if you have thoughts of doing this, check your local code first.

- I used a Taco iSeries 3-way, Reset Mixing Valve for the floor radiant panel. I've had a lot of success with them in the past and I'll always opt for a responsive mixing valve.

- I went with a Caleffi DirtMag even though it's a new system. Someday, it won't be.

- I will also be adding a Taco 0-10vDC boiler pump soon. I told you this thing will always be changing.

- I used an Axiom condensate neutralizing pump because there isn't a floor drain nearby. This was also a first for me and I'm impressed.
- My choice for flushing the system and conditioning the water were the Fernox aerosol products, F1 and F5. Manufacturers are making it easier and easier for us.
- I used CPVC for the entire run of exhaust pipe.
- I painted my gas pipe yellow. I did it for all my commercial customers, so if I can do it for them, I can do it for me.
- I installed a ½" swing check in the makeup water line just before the Caleffi combo fill to eliminate the occasional drip from the backflow preventor. Thank you, Hot Rod, for that tip.
- A temperature gauge in the flue pipe? Yep.
- The red box (most times a concrete pad) beneath the boiler is a staple on all my Knight installations. It matches the color of the control. I told you I was a heating geek, didn't I?
- I installed a 0-60 PSI water gauge on the makeup water line to measure street pressure.

My next step will be adding some radiators with a TRV on each, constant circulation. All of them will be sized so that they can heat the room at the lowest supply water temperature that makes sense. The lower the return water temperature, the longer the boiler is in condensing mode. The longer the boiler is in condensing mode, the more efficient it is.

At some point, I'll also add radiant ceilings, radiant walls, and a towel warmer for wife. Maybe a second boiler too.

Why not? Some guys buy snowmobiles, Harleys, and 120" flat screen TVs.

Not me, I'm a heating geek.

CHAPTER 20 – Ch-Ch-Changes

Turn and face the strange… ch-ch-changes. Bowie nailed it, didn't he? Dylan nailed it too because it certainly feels like the times are a changin' to me.

As I punch these keys using only my two index fingers, we are enduring COVID-19 and my consulting business has slowed WAY down. The phone stopped ringing and the emails stopped coming about five weeks ago. No more load calculations. No more piping diagrams. No more site visits. No more pump sizing. No contractor referrals. Nothing. Nada. Zilch. And the timing could not have been better.

Don't get me wrong, I love what I do, and I'll be doing it until the day that I'm six feet on the wrong side of the sod. Most everything has slowed WAY down so my situation is not abnormal. It's the new normal, for now. Not too many things are normal these days. Up is down. Right is wrong. Fact is fiction. Fiction is fact. And someday, hopefully sooner than later, things will return to some modicum of normalcy.

But for now, these past weeks and months of business downtime has allowed me to focus on some other things that needed my attention whether there was a deadly virus or not.

Life comes at you fast, so you better be ready for it.

What's that old joke?

"How do you make God laugh?"

"Tell him your plans."

It's true. The only constant is change. The best laid plans of mice and men often go astray, some notable poet once said.

For us, my wife Barb and I, it started when her hours were drastically cut, and she started sending out her resume. And by sending it out, I mean sending it way out. Barb and I both grew up in Tinley Park, Illinois. She was my girlfriend in 7th grade and that romance lasted two glorious weeks. A year later, her family relocated to Arizona and that's where she's been until we married 8 years ago. She has two sons and two granddaughters that live in the Las Vegas area and she moved here for, you're not going to believe this, me.

Well, I thought it was time to repay her commitment to me, so I suggested she send the resume to Vegas and its surrounding communities. Long story short, she was offered a good job and she accepted. She is a

Certified Nurse/Midwife and now she has resumed her nursing career after delivering 2000 plus babies as a midwife.

Now, we're in scramble mode. She needed to start her job on May 4th, so we needed to get a home out there stat and move 90% of our stuff out there. We managed that successfully while I remain in the Chicago area until June 6th. That's when the movers come to grab my library of books, my boxes and boxes of vinyl albums, CDs, cassettes, two stereos, and a large inventory of tools that I refuse to lose even though I haven't been a contractor for almost two years now.

The reason I stayed back was because I needed to get our house ready for sale. And by get ready, I mean make it look as good as a state-of-the-art boiler installation. In for a penny, in for a pound, right? My list of things to do started with a count of 53, grew by 15 or 20, and now I've got it whittled down to 3. The house went on the market two days ago, May 26th.

I painted everything on the inside of the house. I removed and packed the Lochinvar boiler and all the near boiler piping I use for training. I cleaned grout. I power washed the deck and driveway. I repaired things that should have been repaired long ago. I was shocked and disappointed in myself by the number of things I put off, not my normal method of operation. I replaced doors and doorknobs. I packed a 500-pound steam radiator from 1865 in a self-made crate that could now survive an earthquake, so I'm hoping it will survive the movers. I installed a new central AC system among so many other things that I do not want to do again for at least another year. I got out of the trenches for a reason.

During all this, we lost my dad. He was my hero and it happened on the same day Barb left for Nevada. He was an incredible guy and I know they say that about most people, but he really was. He grew up in a broken home on Chicago's south side. After a fight with his stepdad, he quit high school and joined the army. He was 17. He earned a Bronze Star and a Purple Heart, and he never talked about the Korean War until he retired, and then, that's all he talked about. It haunted him. He told me stories about events that no teenager should ever have to go through. We ask our young kids to do more than they should, for reasons that often confound us.

He was a war hero. There is no denying that, but that did not define him. What did define him was his words and his actions. That is what defines all of us. What makes us different is the words we choose and the actions we take, and my dad shined in those moments. His honesty, empathy, integrity, character, and work ethic; were remarkable.

He's the man who taught me how to be a man, and I'm not sure where he got that ability. He didn't get it from his dad or his stepdad. His dad left the family when he was baby. His stepdad had a serious drinking problem and was violent when he drank. By the way, his stepdad, my grandfather, never drank again after the fight that sent my dad to Korea. He turned out to be a great guy. My dad must have committed to breaking the cycle of bad dads and boy did he ever. I miss him every day.

It's been almost five weeks since Barb and our dog, Little Man, moved west and I haven't had a minute of down time. I'm lucky in that regard. I know a lot of people that are struggling with the isolation. I've been too busy to feel down. There's not even a TV here now, and I don't miss it one bit. The isolation and the thoughts that run through my mind while working 10-hour days in my own home, have taught me much about myself. It's made me more self-aware. It's also a little disturbing and comical at the same time.

I'm not looking forward to living 1800 miles away from my girls, my granddaughters, my mom, and my friends. But I must be fair to my wife. She deserves it. I'm also not looking forward to the 1800-mile drive, but I am welcoming change.

Lastly, I look forward to getting back to my wife, dog, and the craft of hydronics.

Be safe. Be smart. Be patient. Things will get better.

CHAPTER 21 – Commercial Boilers and CSD-1

The opening paragraphs of any commercial boiler installation manual will inundate you with acronyms, standards, codes, and multiple mentions of the Authority Having Jurisdiction, AHJ. This one is courtesy of Dunkirk Boiler. Sound familiar? I hope so.

Your commercial boiler is furnished with combustion side water or steam controls to meet our interpretation of the American Society of Mechanical Engineers (ASME) Safety Code for Controls and Safety Devices for Automatically Fired Boilers, No. CSD-1.

Installation shall conform to the requirements of the authority having jurisdiction, or, in the absence of such requirements, to the National Fuel Gas Code, ANSI-Z223.1/NFPA-54 (latest revision). Where required by the authority having jurisdiction, the installation shall conform to the American Society of Mechanical Engineers (ASME) Safety Code for Controls and Safety Devices for Automatically Fire Boilers, No. CSD-1.

CSD-1 controls and this installation may be subject to approval by local inspectors. Additional parts or equipment may be required. Consult local authorities having jurisdiction before the installation of the boiler.

CSD-1 controls furnished with commercial boilers are applicable to boilers with inputs above 400,000 Btu/hr. (Models 500-1500)

Additional parts required by CSD-1 Standards may be necessary to make this boiler compliant. This supplemental instruction manual should be used in conjunction with the Installation, Operation and Maintenance manual for your specific boiler.

The AHJ is typically an inspector from the municipality's Building Department. Other times, it's the local Fire Marshal.

If you haven't taken the time to read the CSD-1 Standard, you're going to run into some trouble come inspection time. We're required to follow these rules, so boilers don't blow up and people don't die, and the inspector is both the check and balance in that equation. The way I see it, understand it, and have done it for years goes like this:

I read the boiler manufacturer's instructions.

I review the CSD-1 Standard.

I consider the city that I'm working in, and what they typically require.

And then I move forward. By the way, you can buy a pdf copy of CSD-1, Controls and Safety Devices for Automatically Fired Boilers, online for about a hundred bucks. Inspectors are human too, so if they nail you on something that you don't agree with, you'll be able to have an intelligent conversation with them by being familiar with the document. My goal is to go over some of the highlights as it relates to hot water boilers.

The CSD-1 Standard applies to boilers over 400,000 BTU/h and caps at 12,500,000 BTU/h. At that 12,500 MBH mark, a new Standard applies; NFPA 85 Boiler and Combustion Systems Hazard Code.

In my experience, these are the things that the authority having jurisdiction immediately looks for. The first observation happens before he or she even steps foot in the boiler room. Under CE-110(a) of CSD-1, it states "A manually operated shutdown switch or circuit breaker shall be located just outside the boiler room and marked for easy identification." One guy tried to fail me on this. He was looking for the emergency, red button type switch and it was nowhere to be found. What I did do was clearly identify the circuit breaker right outside the Boiler Room entry as "Boiler" and showed him what was referenced in the document. He wasn't happy about conceding, but he did. Being prepared in that situation paid off for me. I like these emergency switches, but it would have been redundant in this case.

Once inside the Room, their Eagle Eyes scan the workmanship or lack thereof, the cleanliness of the room, serviceability of the boiler, evidence of specific controls they require, and will likely know within the first ten seconds whether you will get their exalted blessing or incur their wrath. Most of the inspectors I've dealt with went in search of the Manual Reset High Limit Control (CW-410) and the Manual Reset Low Water Cutoff (CW-130) right away. My supply houses made that easy for me because they always included each in their quotes for the boilers and they would invariably be a Honeywell L4006E1000 for the Temperature Limit Control and a Taco LFM0243S-1 for the Low Water Cut Off Control.

It's important to note that the Manual Reset Temperature Limit is to be used in conjunction with the automatic reset limit control that comes with the boiler, and is set 5-10 degrees higher so as to prevent nuisance tripping of the manual reset limit. Also, noteworthy, and something they will catch every time, is to make sure there is no isolation valve installed between the LWCO and the boiler (CW-130c). You don't want the control sensing the presence of water when the boiler might not have any. I find the wording of this Standard in CSD-1 to be a bit ambiguous so here's a picture that clarifies things.

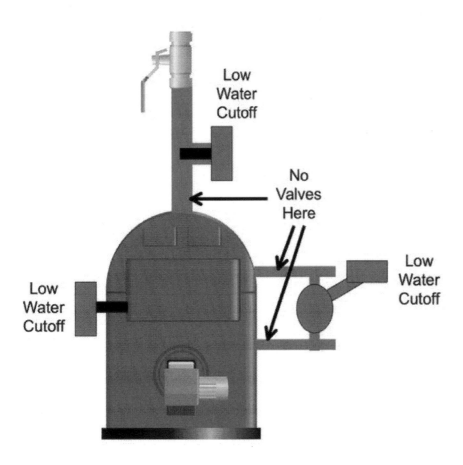

Courtesy of Ray Wohlfarth.

On the visual inspection, the inspector is going to take a mental note and then a physical note on some things that we should be doing on all boiler installations no matter what the BTU/h. A gas piping sediment trap is required and must be at least 3" long and at the bottom of the vertical drop, out the bottom run of the tee. A manually operated gas shut off valve is required and must operate freely without the use of your hammer, channel locks, or 14" steel pipe wrench. It also must be exercised regularly to insure easy operation by hand.

The Pressure Relief Valve on any hot water boilers shall "conform to ASME Section I or IV, as applicable", and be installed on a vertical plane as the picture below shows.

I've seen these valves installed backwards, on a horizontal plane, plugged, or with threads on the bottom of the discharge pipe. The threads on the bottom of the pipe are just an invitation for some unknowing individual to spin a cap on them to stop a dripping valve while creating a potential bomb. I like to use black iron pipe cut raw, and even on an angle sometimes; anything to deter the unknowing from doing the unthinkable.

Once the near boiler piping and controls have been evaluated, the inspector is then likely to take a close look at how the room is getting its combustion air. I'd say 85% of the commercial boilers rooms I've been in have gotten their combustion air from a fixed louver that is now covered by plywood or cardboard and duct tape. Therefore, there are inspectors and fire marshals that will hold building owners, building engineers, and contractors accountable if they're unable to do so by themselves.

I prefer using a motorized damper with an integral end switch in accordance with the combustion air requirements of NFPA 54/ANSIZ223.1, National Fuel Code. This way I don't need to worry about someone blocking the oxygen needed for complete combustion. If the damper doesn't open, the burner circuit is never energized. If the burner doesn't fire up, the contractor's phone rings, and the problem gets solved the right way and nobody gets hurt. It's almost a bullet-proof method of attack.

At the end of the CSD-1 Standard they provide various illustrations of acceptable gas trains with provisions for valve leakage tests. I wouldn't expect gas valves leaking to be a common thing, but the provision is there for a reason.

Testing, servicing, maintaining, and cleaning under this Standard is required and they often defer to the manufacturer's recommendations on that. Proper documentation of all the work done is emphasized throughout CSD-1. This kind of work is not for everyone. This is for heavyweight hydronic techs who take pride in their work while providing the safest possible boiler operation.

For me, spending the hundred bucks for the CSD-1 Standard was worth it. That one instance of circuit breaker versus emergency switch covered the bill. After that it was money in my pocket, not to mention the peace of mind it always gave me to know that it was another job done the right way. It's amazing how much you can distance yourself from the pack just by doing your job...the right way.

CHAPTER 22 - Manual J Simplified

There are plenty of lively conversations on whether it's necessary to do a Manual J Heat Loss Load Calculation for every boiler you replace or install. There's also been a surplus of articles written on this topic with an equal amount of opinions. This is not about my opinion whether you should do one or not but, for the record, I've done one on every job going back to the early 2000's. Prior to that, it was about 50/50. To me it makes sense, but you do you.

What I'd like to share is the fact that doing a load calculation manually isn't that hard and the more you do, the quicker you'll get. You'll find ways to streamline the process and develop an easy method of operation to get it done. You'll learn early on that one simple math mistake quickly becomes a compounding error as it effects the numbers thereafter. Trust me, you won't make that mistake often because it's a pain to correct.

The front page of Manual J is made up of job information, design conditions, a heating summary, a cooling summary, an equipment summary, and construction data. At the start, you'll just need to fill out the Job Information, Design Conditions, and Construction Data. **Design Conditions**, if you don't already know yours, can be found in Table 1 Outdoor Design Conditions, on Page 51 of Manual J. I lived in the Chicago area up until a couple months ago, so I always used -4° F as my **Outdoor Design Temperature.** My **Indoor Design Temperature** was typically 70° F, but that had the potential to vary if I knew enough about the people who lived there and they intended to keep living there.

There are 19 horizontal line items on the ACCA Manual J worksheet and as many columns as needed for a room by room analysis. Of those 19 lines, you can eliminate lines 7, 14, 16, 17, 18, and 19 right off the bat for purposes of sizing a boiler. Those lines deal with heat gain and boiler guys need not be concerned with heat gain. That's for the AC and psychometrics crowd.

Line Number 1 is as easy as it gets, so we'll only spend two sentences on it. **Name of Room**, you got this.

Line Number 2 is asking for **Running Foot of Exposed Wall**. An exposed wall is defined as any wall that butts up to an unheated area, usually the outdoors. Unheated garages and knee walls would also fit the description. At this point we're not concerned with the area of the wall, just the length of it.

Line Number 3 is simply the **Room Dimensions** in length and width.

Line Number 4 asks for the **Ceiling Height** of each room.

Everything we've done so far is relatively easy, but we also need to be sure those numbers are accurate because it will come back to haunt us a few lines down if they're not. Between Lines 4 and 5, the headings for each column change. Type of Exposure, Construction Number, Heating HTM (Heat Transfer Multiplier), Area, and Heating BTU/h are some new terms we need to get familiar with.

Type of Exposure is straightforward. Exposed walls, windows, doors, ceilings, and floors are the surfaces that account for the building's heat loss. Each type of exposure within your building will be assigned a ***Construction Number.*** The Construction Number is an alpha-numeric designation that can be found in Table 2 - Heat Transfer Multipliers (Heating) starting on page 65. It is based on the type of construction of the window, door, wall, ceiling, or floor. For instance, if a particular window is wood framed, double pane with Low E glass, and your **Design Delta T** is 80° F, you would go to Table 2, No. 3D, and where that line intersects 80° Winter Temperature difference is your Heat Transfer Multiplier (HTM). In this case, that HTM 28.9 and will find out how we use that shortly.

Line Number 5 requires us to provide the **Gross Exposed Walls and Partitions**. For this, we multiply the Running Foot Exposed Wall found on Line 2 by the Ceiling Height found on Line 4.

Line 2 x Line 4 = Line 5
*Any shaded block on the Manual J Worksheet remains blank, as is.

Line Number 6 deals exclusively with heat loss of **Windows and Glass Doors**. It's exactly as I described above with two additional steps. On Line 6a under the column Const. No., we write 3D as our reference. On that same line under column HTM Heating, we write 28.9. Staying on the same line, we move over to first room column under area. Let's say the square footage of the windows, of that construction, in that room is 70. Are we good so far? Now, we take the HTM of 28.9 and multiply it by the area of the glass 70.
28.9 x 70 = 2023 BTU/h loss for those specific windows.

Line Number 7? **Forget about it. It's not for Boiler Guys.**

Line Number 8 is essentially the same as Line Number 6 but only deals with doors that aren't glass. Easy enough, right?

Line Number 9 is for **Net Exposed Walls and Partitions**. The first step here is to go back to Table 2 for the Construction Number and Heating HTM and post those numbers in the appropriate columns. Our walls in this case is 10" masonry with no insulation and unfinished. This is not as atypical as it seems. It's fairly common in basement walls above grade. The Construction Number would 14A, while the HTM for an 80° Delta T would be a whopping 40.8. The square footage of this exposed basement wall is 281. Now we do the math just like in previous steps.
40.8 x 281 = 11,465 BTU/h loss through this wall.

To this point, we've ignored Line 7 because it deals only with heat gain and we've completed the other eight steps based on information we've gathered from the jobsite or a blueprint. We know the information is reliable because we were precise in gathering it. It's also important to note that Manual J is very specific on how these measurements of doors and windows are taken. They provide detailed information and plenty of sketches to drive home the point so be sure to pick up a copy.

Line Numbers 10 and 11 are for **Ceilings** and **Floors** respectively and are to be completed using the same methods used in Lines 6 and 8.

Line Number 12 is where things tend to get a little tricky. **Heat Loss due to Infiltration** is almost always an estimate and at best, using a blower door test, is still like trying to hit a moving target. Pressures inside and outside the envelope are part and parcel to the equation when determining infiltration and both are rarely steady. For the sake of this conversation, I'm going to use the estimated method used in Manual J which makes some assumptions outlined in Appendix A-5.

Looking at Table 5 below, you'll see that were given some ACH values based on the building size and the quality of construction. Once you determine the ACH, you plug that number into the first equation, do the math, and arrive at the CFM. Then, plug the CFM into the next equation and the answer to that will give you BTU/h. Plug that answer into the last equation which will give you the elusive HTM for the window(s) and door(s) infiltration. As you can see in photo, Lines 6a, 6b, 6c, and 8 are added together to give us a total of 222 square feet which is then multiplied by the HTM of 70.6 which results in a total heat loss of 15,673 BTU/h for windows and doors. And that same procedure is used along Line 12 for room by room heat loss due to infiltration.

Table 5 – Manual J Winter Infiltration

Winter Air Changes per Hour (ACH)

Envelope	900sf or Less	900-1500sf	1500-2100sf	Over 2100sf

Best – (<.25 CFM/Lin. Ft.) ACH	0.4 ACH	0.4 ACH	0.3 ACH	0.3
Avg. – (.25-.50 CFM/Lin. Ft.) ACH	1.2 ACH	1.0 ACH	0.8 ACH	0.7
Poor – (>.50 CFM/Lin. Ft.) ACH	2.2 ACH	1.6 ACH	1.2 ACH	1.0

Fireplace Notes

Best – Add 0.1 for each fireplace. Combustion air from the outside and tight glass doors.

Average – Add 0.2 for each fireplace. Combustion air from inside and tight glass doors.

Poor – Add 0.6 for each fireplace. Combustion air from the inside and no glass doors.

Winter Infiltration HTM Calculation

ACH x Cubic Feet x 0.0167^* = _____CFM

1.1^{**} x CFM x Winter Design Delta T = _____BTU/h

BTU/h ÷ Total Window and Door Area = _____HTM

*0.0167 is a constant and is the decimal equivalent of 1/60.

**1.1 is a constant and represents the amount of BTU required to heat 1 cubic foot of water, 1°F.

Think of this as a reference or quick summary to ACCA's Manual J Residential Load Calculations. The book is about 125 pages long, 75 of those pages are tables and appendices you'll need to reference in or order to complete the work. After doing a year's worth of Heat Loss Load Calculations, those 75 pages of pulp nonfiction will be well worn, and you will have taken another giant step in distancing yourself from the competition.

Load Calculations done via software are easier and quicker. You can easily manipulate numbers which then change the values down the line accordingly, but I think its important to understand what these numbers represent and where they come from. Software can also generate detailed reports, graphs, charts, and even material lists at times. I still do it both ways. I like to compare results when the same information is being used.

FIGURE 3-3 EXAMPLE HEAT LOSS CALCULATION
DO NOT WRITE IN SHADED BLOCKS

					Entire House			1 Living			2 Dining			3 Laundry			4 Kitchen			5 Bath - 1		
1	Name of Room																					
2	Running Ft. Exposed Wall				160			21			25			18			11			9		
3	Room Dimensions Ft.				51 x 29			21 x 14			7 x 18			7 x 11			11 x 11			9 x 11		
4	Ceiling Ht. Ft Directions Room Faces				8			8 West			8 North			8			8 East			8 East		
	TYPE OF EXPOSURE	Const. No.	HTM Htg.	HTM Clg.	Area or Length	Btuh Htg.	Btuh Clg.	Area or Length	Btuh Htg.	Btuh Clg.	Area or Length	Btuh Htg.	Btuh Clg.	Area or Length	Btuh Htg.	Btuh Clg.	Area or Length	Btuh Htg.	Btuh Clg.	Area or Length	Btuh Htg.	Btuh Clg.
5	Gross a	12-d			1280			168			200			144			88			72		
	Exposed b	14-b			480																	
	Walls & c	15-b			800																	
	Partitions d																					
6	Windows a	3-A	41.3		60	2478		40	1652		20	826										
	& Glass b	2-C	48.8		20	976																
	Doors Htg. c	2-A	35.6		105	3738											11	392		8	285	
	d																					
7	Windows North																					
	& Glass E&W																					
	Doors Clg. South																					
8	Other Doors	11-E	14.3		37	529								17	243							
9	Net a	12-d	6.0		1078	6468		128	768		180	1080		127	762		77	462		64	384	
	Exposed b	14-b	10.8		460	4968																
	Walls & c	15-b	5.5		800	4400																
	Partitions d																					
10	Ceilings a	16-d	4.0		1479	5916		294	1176		126	504		77	308		121	484		99	396	
	b																					
11	Floors a	21-a	1.8		1479	2662																
	b																					
12	Infiltration HTM		70.6		222	15673		40	2824		20	1412		17	1200		11	777		8	565	
13	Sub Total Btuh Loss =6+8+9+10+11+12					47808			6420			3822			2513			2115			1630	
14	Duct Btuh Loss		0%			—			—			—			—			—				
15	Total Btuh Loss = 13 + 14					47808			6420			3822			2513			2115			1630	
16	People @ 300 & Appliances 1200																					
17	Sensible Btuh Gain =7+8+9+10+11+12+16																					
18	Duct Btuh Gain %																					
19	Total Sensible Gain = 17 + 18																					

From Table 2

ASSUMED DESIGN CONDITIONS AND CONSTRUCTION (Heating):	Const. No.	HTM
A. Determing Outside Design Temperature -5° db-Table 1		
B. Select Inside Design Temperature 70° db		
C. Design Temperature Difference: 75 Degrees		
D. Windows: Living Room & Dining Room - Clear Fixed Glass, Double Glazed - Wood Frame - Table 2 .	3A	41.3
Basement - Clear Glass Metal Casement Windows, with Storm - Table 2	2C	48.8
Others - Double Hung, Clear, Single Glass and Storm, Wood Frame - Table 2	2A	35.6
E. Doors: Metal, Urethane Core, no Storm - Table 2	11E	14.3
F. First Floor Walls: Basic Frame Construction with ½" Asphalt Board (R-11) - Table 2	12d	6.0
Basement wall: 8" Concrete Block - Table 2		
Above Grade Height: 3 ft (R = 5)	14b	10.8
Below Grade Height: 5 ft (R = 5)	15b	5.5
G. Ceiling: Basic Construction Under Vented Attic with Insulation (R-19) - Table 2.	16d	4.0
H. Floor: Basement Floor, 4" Concrete - Table 2	21a	1.8

I. All moveable windows and doors have certified leakage of 0.5 CFM per running foot of crack (without storm), envelope has plastic vapor barrier and major cracks and penetrations have been sealed with caulking material, no fireplace, all exhausts and vents are dampered, all ducts taped.

23

Made in the USA
Monee, IL
20 October 2020